# The Rise of the Pasdaran

## Assessing the Domestic Roles of Iran's Islamic Revolutionary Guards Corps

Frederic Wehrey, Jerrold D. Green, Brian Nichiporuk, Alireza Nader, Lydia Hansell, Rasool Nafisi, S. R. Bohandy

Prepared for the Office of the Secretary of Defense

Approved for public release; distribution unlimited

NATIONAL DEFENSE RESEARCH INSTITUTE

The research described in this report was prepared for the Office of the Secretary of Defense (OSD). The research was conducted in the RAND National Defense Research Institute, a federally funded research and development center sponsored by the OSD, the Joint Staff, the Unified Combatant Commands, the Department of the Navy, the Marine Corps, the defense agencies, and the defense Intelligence Community under Contract W74V8H-06-C-0002.

**Library of Congress Cataloging-in-Publication Data** is available for this publication.

ISBN 978-0-8330-4620-8

The RAND Corporation is a nonprofit research organization providing objective analysis and effective solutions that address the challenges facing the public and private sectors around the world. RAND's publications do not necessarily reflect the opinions of its research clients and sponsors. **RAND®** is a registered trademark.

Published 2009 by the RAND Corporation
1776 Main Street, P.O. Box 2138, Santa Monica, CA 90407-2138
1200 South Hayes Street, Arlington, VA 22202-5050
4570 Fifth Avenue, Suite 600, Pittsburgh, PA 15213-2665
RAND URL: http://www.rand.org/
To order RAND documents or to obtain additional information, contact
Distribution Services: Telephone: (310) 451-7002;
Fax: (310) 451-6915; Email: order@rand.org

# Preface

The purpose of this research is to assess the broad-ranging domestic roles of Iran's Islamic Revolutionary Guards Corps (IRGC), also known as the Pasdaran (Persian for "Guards"), to determine the full scope of its influence over Iran's political culture, economy, and society. The study analyzed the institution's ideological outreach to the Iranian populace through education, training, and media; its ascendancy in Iran's strategic business sectors; and its role in Iran's factionalized political landscape. The research team paid particular attention to instances in which the IRGC's ascendancy has provoked dissent from certain population segments, as well as cases in which it has mobilized and broadened its circle of constituents. This monograph concludes by offering potential trajectories for the IRGC's involvement in Iranian politics, as well as its own institutional evolution, which appears to be increasingly beset by factionalism. In addition, the document outlines a future research agenda for the study of the IRGC that draws comparative insights from analyses of the Pakistani and Chinese militaries. This research should be of interest to analysts and policymakers concerned with Iranian domestic politics and strategic behavior, as well as those interested, more broadly, in comparative studies of civil-military relations.

This research was conducted within the Intelligence Policy Center of the RAND National Defense Research Institute, a federally funded research and development center sponsored by the Office of the Secretary of Defense, the Joint Staff, the Unified Combatant Commands, the Department of the Navy, the Marine Corps, the defense agencies, and the defense Intelligence Community.

For more information on RAND's Intelligence Policy Center, contact the Director, John Parachini. He can be reached by email at John_Parachini@rand.org; by phone at 703-413-1100, extension 5579; or by mail at the RAND Corporation, 1200 South Hayes Street, Arlington, Virginia 22202-5050. More information about RAND is available at www.rand.org.

# Contents

Preface ................................................................. iii

Figures ................................................................. ix

Summary ................................................................. xi

Acknowledgments ........................................................ xix

Abbreviations .......................................................... xxi

CHAPTER ONE

Introduction ............................................................ 1

CHAPTER TWO

The IRGC in Context: Iran's Security and Political Landscape ........ 7

The IRGC in Iran's Security Hierarchy .............................. 8

Iran's Factional Landscape ......................................... 13

CHAPTER THREE

The IRGC's Diverse Domestic Roles: Origins and Evolution .......... 19

Postrevolutionary Developments: Consolidating Internal Control ....... 20

The Sacred Defense: The IRGC in the Iran-Iraq War .................. 23

"Popularizing" the IRGC: The Development of the Basij Resistance
    Force ........................................................... 25

The Guardians of the Revolution: The IRGC's Domestic Intelligence
    and Security Roles .............................................. 29

The Merger of Basij and IRGC: A Sign of the Regime's Growing
    Entrenchment .................................................... 32

CHAPTER FOUR

**Militarizing Civil Society: The IRGC's Indoctrination, Training, and Media Activities** ....................................................... 35

The IRGC's Ideological Activism: Origins and Development .............. 35

The IRGC Presence in Iran's Education System ........................... 38

The "Ten-Million-Man Army": The IRGC's Role in Popular
  Paramilitary Training ..................................................... 44

  Increasing the Basij's Capability to Conduct Asymmetric Homeland
    Defense ................................................................. 45

  Disaster-Relief Training ................................................. 47

  Protection Against Soft Coups ........................................... 47

  Additional Cultural Education ........................................... 48

The IRGC Media Apparatus: Formal and Informal Influences ............ 49

Censorship of Independent Media Outlets ................................ 53

CHAPTER FIVE

**Economic Expansion: The IRGC's Business Conglomerate and
  Public Works** ............................................................ 55

Origins of the IRGC's Economic Activities ................................ 56

Foundations (Bonyads) .................................................... 57

Construction, Engineering, and Manufacturing Companies ................ 59

Illicit and Black Market Activities ....................................... 64

Public Works .............................................................. 66

The Dilemmas of Economic Expansion ................................... 70

CHAPTER SIX

**The IRGC in Politics** .................................................... 77

The Origins of the IRGC as a Political Force ............................. 77

Ideological Factionalism Inside the IRGC ................................ 81

Possible Future Scenarios for the IRGC .................................. 89

  Scenario 1: The Evolving Role of the Supreme Leader and the
    Eventual Succession to Khamenei ...................................... 89

  Scenario 2: The "Muslim Reza Khan" ................................... 90

  Scenario 3: The Religious Turkish Option, or a "Coup by
    Memorandum" ......................................................... 91

**CHAPTER SEVEN**
**Conclusion: Toward a More Strategic Understanding of the IRGC** ...93
The Utility of a Comparative Approach: Pakistan and China............. 94

**APPENDIXES**
**A. Business Organizations Affiliated with the IRGC or Influenced**
   **by IRGC Personnel**........................................................ 99
**B. Current and Former IRGC Personnel**............................... 103
**C. Evolution of the Islamic Republic and the IRGC**................... 109
**D. Provincial Map of Iran**.................................................. 113
**E. Glossary of Persian Terms**............................................. 115

**Bibliography**................................................................ 117

# Figures

2.1.    Iran's National Security Establishment ........................... 9
C.1.    Timeline of the Islamic Republic of Iran and the IRGC ..... 110
D.1.    Provincial Map of Iran .......................................... 113

# Summary

Founded by a decree from Ayatollah Khomeini shortly after the victory of the 1978–1979 Islamic Revolution, Iran's Islamic Revolutionary Guards Corps (IRGC) has evolved well beyond its original foundations as an ideological guard for the nascent revolutionary regime. Today, the IRGC functions as an expansive socio-political-economic conglomerate whose influence extends into virtually every corner of Iranian political life and society. Bound together by the shared experience of war and the socialization of military service, the Pasdaran have articulated a populist, authoritarian, and assertive vision for the Islamic Republic of Iran that they maintain is a more faithful reflection of the revolution's early ideals.

The IRGC's presence is particularly powerful in Iran's highly factionalized political system, in which the president, much of the cabinet, many members of parliament, and a range of other provincial and local administrators hail from the ranks of the IRGC. Outside the political realm, the IRGC oversees a robust apparatus of media resources, training activities, and education programs designed to bolster loyalty to the regime, prepare the citizenry for homeland defense, and burnish its own institutional credibility vis-à-vis other factional actors. It is in the economic sphere, however, that the IRGC has seen the greatest growth and diversification—strategic industries and commercial services ranging from dam and pipeline construction to automobile manufacturing and laser eye surgery have fallen under its sway, along with a number of illicit smuggling and black-market enterprises.

Taken in sum, these attributes argue for a reexamination of the IRGC, less as a traditional military entity wielding a navy, ground forces, air force, and a clandestine paramilitary wing (the Qods Force) and more as a domestic actor, albeit one that is not monolithic and is itself beset by internal differences and factionalism. Certainly, elements of Iran's military forces present worrisome threats to U.S. strategy, most notably in the areas of asymmetric naval tactics, intermediate-range ballistic missiles, and support for terrorism. But to policymakers and analysts concerned with the broader trajectory of the Islamic Republic of Iran—the internal roots of its external behavior and the sources of its durability and weakness—the IRGC may be more profitably viewed as a deeply entrenched domestic institution. Arguably, this internal role overshadows its significance as a purely military force.

With this in mind, this monograph assesses the extent of the IRGC's penetration into Iran's society, economy, and politics. We begin by situating the IRGC within the context of Iran's factional landscape and security bureaucracy, highlighting the origins and early development of its domestic roles. Next, we cover the IRGC's role in popular paramilitary training, higher education, the indoctrination of youth, and its influence over Iran's domestic media. This extensive apparatus serves both the regime's interests—mobilizing the population into a "10 million–man army" for the defense of the homeland and countering reform activism, particularly on university campuses—and the more parochial goal of blunting any criticism of Pasdaran nepotism and economic corruption. We then discuss the IRGC's economic role. We survey its broad-ranging business interests in numerous Iranian market sectors, as well as its role in public works, highlighting how these activities lend the institution a multidimensional quality. Finally, we conclude with an assessment of the IRGC as a political actor, paying special attention to emerging factionalism within its ranks and highlighting instances in which these fissures have surfaced in the past.

From these lines of inquiry, the following conclusions emerge and have implications for future U.S. analysis and policy toward the IRGC and the Islamic Republic of Iran writ large.

**The IRGC is but one actor in Iran's security and factional landscape whose influence is exerted informally.** Within Iran's security hierarchy, the IRGC frequently vies with other security organs, such as the Ministry of Intelligence and Security (MOIS), Ministry of the Interior, and Law Enforcement Forces (LEF), for visibility, power, and influence. This rivalry may shed light on IRGC actions that appear at first glance to be detrimental to the larger interests of the state. Moreover, much of the IRGC's ascendancy has been facilitated by the complex structure of the Iranian political system, which results in a default drift toward informality in decisionmaking. At the same time, the IRGC's informal influence is subject to the same factional fissures that define the broader political spectrum—among conservative traditionalists, conservative pragmatists, radicals, and reformists. Similarly, although other security organs and institutions of power may be staffed by former Pasdaran, it does not follow that these individuals act in lockstep with the corporate interests of the IRGC—office-holding tends to generate its own set of priorities that can offset even the powerful social bonds and ideology imparted by military service.

**The IRGC has attempted to cultivate legitimacy today by burnishing its role in the Iran-Iraq War and the postwar reconstruction; this early history has been a matter of factional contention and public ambivalence.** Understanding the IRGC's early history and, particularly, its expansion and deviation from the role envisioned for it by the Islamic Republic's founders is critical to discerning its future trajectory. Much of the institution's rise to prominence over competing militias and paramilitaries in the postrevolutionary period was due to its effectiveness in suppressing internal dissent. Similarly, many in the IRGC's leadership saw the Iran-Iraq War as a mechanism to consolidate their internal position and marginalize the regular forces politically—goals that may have taken precedence over matters of military strategy.

Today, the IRGC is attempting to trumpet its role in the "sacred defense" of the Islamic Republic of Iran during the "imposed war." Its current mobilization of the populace against both internal and external enemies is, in some sense, a reenactment of this period. Similarly, IRGC leaders frequently point to their service in Iran's postwar reconstruction to justify the IRGC's current expansion into new business sectors. These themes are being contested by competing factions and the public alike. Anecdotal reports suggest that many in the Iranian public offer a radically different interpretation of the IRGC's wartime performance, believing that the IRGC's excessive zealotry and *nadanan kari* (inexperience) prevented the complete battlefield defeat of Iraqi forces.

**Although well developed and extensive, the IRGC's efforts at popular mobilization and indoctrination have met with mixed results. There appears to be an urban-rural split in public views toward the IRGC.** Part of its foundational mandate, the IRGC's role in indoctrination and ideological outreach to the Iranian public has taken on a new urgency, given the regime's heightened threat perception—particularly from a U.S.-sponsored "velvet revolution," i.e., the erosion of revolutionary ideals via civil-society organizations and ethnic dissent. To combat this, the IRGC relies extensively on its poorly trained popular auxiliary, the Basij Resistance Force, whose command structure was formally merged with the IRGC's in 2007. The Basij's role in the Iran-Iraq War—characterized by sheer numbers, youth, and ideological fervor—set the template for the regime's homeland defense strategy today, which relies on partisan warfare against an invading force by a populace that has been mobilized and indoctrinated by the IRGC. The key unknown is the populace's receptivity to this training and even the commitment of the Basij itself, as monthly training is often a prerequisite for societal benefits, such as loans and scholarships.

In tandem with this paramilitary training, the IRGC exerts its ideological influence through its own media outlets, including Web sites and periodicals that highlight its positive contributions to Iranian society, which include disaster relief, drug interdiction, and rural infrastructure development. Similarly, the IRGC has a presence in Iranian higher education—both through its own affiliate universities and through campus organizations, such as the Lecturers' Basij Organization (LBO) and the Student Basij Organization (SBO). The latter is particularly focused on mitigating student reform activism, although it has been only partly successful in this effort.

Finally, public perceptions of the IRGC appear split between urban areas, where it is seen as the regime's shock-troop force for quelling dissent and enforcing strict social mores, and rural areas, where its construction projects and promises of upward mobility through training have induced a more favorable view among certain marginalized population segments.

**By expanding its business interests and control of the "shadow economy," the IRGC runs the risk of provoking a backlash or diluting its own cohesion.** From laser eye surgery and construction to automobile manufacturing and real estate, the IRGC has extended its influence into virtually every sector of the Iranian market. More than any other aspect of its domestic involvement, the IRGC's business activities embody the institution's multidimensional nature. The commercialization of the IRGC has the potential to broaden its circle of constituents by co-opting financial elites into its constellation of subsidiary companies and subcontractors. At the same time, the monopolization of key sectors has displaced competitors. The key IRGC affiliate in both dynamics is the engineering firm Khatam al-Anbia, which has been awarded more than 750 contracts in various construction, infrastructure, oil, and gas projects. Outside of its declared enterprises, the IRGC is reported to control an underground shadow economy of black-market goods, smuggled into Iran via illegal jetties and other entry points that it alone controls. Reports of dissent against the IRGC's institutional aggrandizement and the personal enrichment of its officers remain fragmentary. According to one Western diplomat resident in Iran from 2003 to 2006,

> There is no bazaari backlash at this point. The general population doesn't know about the IRGC's illegal jetties, the Caspian Sea villas, and their Swiss bank accounts.[1]

What is indisputable is that the IRGC's growing economic might has increased its sense of political privilege and entitlement. Nowhere is this more apparent than in its abrupt closure of the newly opened Imam Khomeini Airport in May 2004 and its ejection of a Turkish firm that had been contracted to administer the airport's opera-

---

[1] Authors' discussion with a Western diplomat based in Tehran from 2003 to 2006, Los Angeles, California, July 18, 2007.

tions, reportedly because the IRGC's own firm had lost the contract. Similarly, the IRGC's elite appeared to ignore an injunction from the Supreme Leader to privatize their holdings—a significant development that could portend the IRGC moving closer to becoming an effective counterauthority to the Supreme Leader. At the same time, its expansion into the business sector runs the risk of spurring internal fractionalization and a dilution of its profession identity.

**As a political actor, the IRGC is susceptible to factional debates—between dogmatic and more pragmatic currents and over the opportunity costs inflicted by Iran's isolation.** The issue of the politicization of the IRGC has been hotly contested, with opposing voices marshaling the authority of Ayatollah Khomeini, who, in many respects, appeared to emulate the views of the former shah in his wariness of the army's interference in politics. Generally marginalized during the Rafsanjani era, the IRGC emerged as political force during the Khatami era when they forged a de facto alliance with conservatives seeking to displace the reformists. Today, the IRGC's political muscle manifests itself in diverse ways—from Basij intimidation of voters to the presence of an ex-IRGC officer as the Deputy Minister of the Interior, responsible for ballot validation and counting in the March 2008 Majles (parliamentary) elections. Nonetheless, as mentioned previously, the IRGC itself is beset with political factionalism, which surfaced even in the election of Mahmoud Ahmadinejad, whose real constituents were lower-ranking Basij rather than the IRGC writ large. Earlier incidents revealed fissures along different lines; for example, the 1994 Qazvin riots, in which locally garrisoned IRGC commanders refused to fire on protestors, revealed that the parochial identities of ethnicity and locale still pervade the IRGC's institutional culture. The Khatami era highlighted the lack of ideological uniformity between the IRGC senior leadership, which supported the conservatives, and the rank-and-file, who were more sympathetic to the reformists.

Most recently, splits have emerged over the economic opportunity costs and hardships incurred by Ahmadinejad's administration, with retired IRGC Brigadier General Mohammad Baqer Qalibaf emerging as a prominent voice by appearing to articulate a more pragmatic path that tries to reconcile ideological steadfastness with economic progress.

Qalibaf's 2005 presidential slogan was "Iranians have a right to the good life," and he has openly made the startling assertion that Iran needs an "Islamist Mohammad Reza Khan." Other IRGC figures who might be termed "pragmatic conservatives" include former Supreme National Security Council (SNSC) chief Ali Larijani and ex-IRGC commander Mohsen Rezai, whose Web site, Tabnak, showcased strong critiques of Ahmadinejad.

**Despite this risk of fractionalization, there are several potential scenarios for the IRGC's elite to consolidate their control over a post-Khamenei Iran.** The death of Supreme Leader Ayatollah Ali Khamenei will present an opportunity for the Pasdaran elite to buttress their institutional primacy and erode the position of rivals. One path to accomplish this would be to influence the appointment of a pliant, figurehead Supreme Leader who would grant a broad berth to the IRGC without any evident breaching of the constitution. Another scenario for the IRGC's consolidation includes the installation of a non-clerical military leader who, while not completely abandoning the precepts of Islamism, would place a greater emphasis on technocratic competence and economic progress. A variant of this trajectory and one that would harness the populace's growing weariness with the regime's top-down religiosity and clerical mismanagement is an overt assumption of power by the IRGC—what might be termed the "religious Turkish model." The focus here would be on the IRGC's promises to clean up politics, fight corruption, and improve Iran's economy.

**The IRGC's domestic ascendancy is not unique, nor is its future trajectory immutable; in both respects, the IRGC can be profitably compared with the militaries of Pakistan and China.** As its history has shown, the IRGC is subject to the same worldly pitfalls and evolutionary mutations that affect other bureaucracies—and this will only intensify as the IRGC delves deeper into profit-making financial activities. Indeed, from this observation, there is benefit in comparing the IRGC's past and future with the evolution of the Pakistani military and Chinese People's Liberation Army (PLA).

The parallels to Pakistan are particularly striking. The Pakistani military runs the country's largest construction consortium, which undertakes rural infrastructure projects and is also heavily involved in such diverse subsidiary enterprises as gas stations, commercial plazas, and poultry farms. There are also a number of military-owned "charitable foundations" that oversee 100 companies involved in banking, insurance, education, and information technology. This expansion has reached such proportions that one scholar has coined the term "Milbus" (military-business) to describe it. One important conclusion emerging from the Pakistani case that has implications for Iran is that the largest supporters of the Pakistani military's economic preeminence are those who might intuitively be assumed to oppose it in favor of a more liberal, free-market approach—the middle classes.

The case of the PLA, however, provides the clearest model for exploring the tensions between economic aggrandizement and military professionalism that are certain to accompany the IRGC's future evolution. Although the PLA, since its origins in the 1920s, had always enjoyed a degree of economic self-sufficiency, by the late 1980s its profit-making enterprises had grown considerably: PLA-owned companies dominated the farming, transportation, information technology, and entertainment sectors. Responding to this, in 1998 the government of Jiang Zemin made the remarkable decision to force the divestiture of the PLA from all of its business activities. The reasons for this move stemmed principally from the civilian leadership's perception that the corruption and black-marketeering that had accompanied the PLA's economic rise had reached intolerable levels, to the point that they were negatively affecting popular perceptions of the Chinese Communist Party. Similarly, the civilian leadership perceived that the military's financial pursuits were proving deleterious to its professionalism, morale, meritocracy, and ability to modernize. Finally, the PLA's businesses had become increasingly decentralized and provincially based, raising fears in the central government of a return to the regional autonomy that defined the prerevolutionary warlord era.

All of this suggests that, in the case of Iran, the expansion and primacy of the IRGC as a political-economic actor will not go unchallenged and that there are inherent limits to whatever symbiosis occurs between civilian elites and military-run business ventures, particularly when these financial activities are perceived to be detrimental to the state's larger national security interests.

# Acknowledgments

We are grateful to our project sponsor for the opportunity to pursue this research and for his supportive and constructive feedback throughout the effort. Numerous RAND colleagues aided our understanding of the IRGC as a domestic actor within the Islamic Republic of Iran, and we thank them for their insights: David Thaler, David Ochmanek, Bruce Pirnie, Derek Eaton, James Dobbins, and Dalia Dassa Kaye. Others provided useful comparative insights, drawing from their expertise in civil-military relations in China, Pakistan, the former Soviet Union, and Turkey. These include Peter A. Wilson, Theodore Karasik, Stephen Larrabee, and Roger Cliff. We owe particular thanks to Lauren Skrabala, Donna Mead, Pamela Orient, Judy Bearer, Terri Perkins, Mary Wrazen, and Sandy Petitjean for their help and efficiency in the final editing and production of this monograph.

Outside RAND, we thank Mark Gorwitz, whose research identified a multitude of extremely helpful sources. During various RAND conferences on Iran, a number of non-U.S. scholars provided us with fresh and illuminating perspectives on the IRGC. And finally, we thank our numerous Iranian interlocutors—both inside and outside the Islamic Republic—who must go unnamed.

# Abbreviations

| | |
|---|---|
| AJO | Agricultural Jihad Organization |
| IRGC | Islamic Revolutionary Guards Corps |
| IRIB | Islamic Republic of Iran Broadcasting |
| IRNA | Islamic Republic of Iran News Agency |
| IRP | Islamic Republic Party |
| LBO | Lecturers' Basij Organization |
| LEF | Law Enforcement Forces |
| MEK | Mujahideen-e Khalq |
| MJF | Mostazafan and Janbazan Foundation |
| MOIS | Ministry of Intelligence and Security |
| OCD | Office for Consolidating Democracy |
| PLA | People's Liberation Army (Chinese) |
| SBO | Student Basij Organization |
| SNSC | Supreme National Security Council |

# CHAPTER ONE

# Introduction

Never solely a military organization in the traditional sense, Iran's Islamic Revolutionary Guards Corps (IRGC)—also known as the Pasdaran (Persian for "guards")—has seen a significant expansion and diversification of its domestic roles since the election of President Mahmoud Ahmadinejad in 2005. Today in Iran, a significant portion of the leadership consists of IRGC veterans, including Ahmadinejad, members of parliament, and most of the cabinet.[1] Bound together by the shared experience of war and the socialization of military service, the IRGC and its veterans have articulated a vision for the Islamic Republic of Iran that can be roughly described as technocratic, populist, authoritarian, highly nationalistic, and—in some cases—anticlerical. These tenets have informed the institution's increasingly assertive influence over Iranian political life—exerted through both formal and informal channels—as well as its administration of a vast network of indoctrination, training, and media activities. Moreover, current and former Pasdaran are present in virtually every sector of the Iranian market, controlling strategic industries and commercial services ranging from dam construction and automobile manufacturing to real estate and laser eye

---

[1] Jamshid Asadi, "Eghtesad-e Rantkhari Dar Iran" (Rent-seeking economy in Iran), Talashonline, no date; Behrouz Khaligh, "Mogheiyate Sepah Pasdaran va Rohaniyat dar sakht-e Ghodrat: Taghyirat dar sakhtar-e siasi-e jomhouri-e eslami, gozar as eligareshi rohaniyat be eligareshi rohaniyat va sepah" (IRGC's position in the power structure of the Islamic Republic: From power of clerics to power of clerics and military), Akhbar-Rooz, July 11, 2006b; Presidency of the Islamic Republic of Iran, Cabinet of Mahmoud Ahmadinejad, 2007.

surgery.[2] Taken in sum, these attributes have apparently empowered the IRGC to become what one longtime analyst has described as "the only institution in Iran capable of both enforcing and breaching any red lines."[3]

Despite this domestic ascendancy, most of the attention currently being paid to the Pasdaran in the West is focused squarely on the IRGC's external, international activities. For example, much has been written in the open press about the involvement of the IRGC's clandestine wing, the Qods Force, in fomenting unrest in southern Iraq, its training of Hezbollah cadres in Lebanon, and its planning of terrorist attacks on Western interests from Beirut to Buenos Aires. Some commentators have also tried to highlight the IRGC's involvement with and alleged control over Iran's nuclear research and weapons program. More recently, the spotlight has been cast on the IRGC's confrontational naval posture toward coalition and U.S. vessels in the Persian Gulf. Observers who do address the IRGC's domestic functions often do so with the implicit assumption that its seemingly hegemonic presence in Iranian political life, along with its rapidly expanding business enterprises and control of Iran's shadow economy, lend it a mafia-like quality that is unique in the world today. As noted by Iranian dissident Mohsen Sazegara, also one of the IRGC's founders, "I don't know of any other organization in any country like the Revolutionary Guards. It's something like the Communist Party, the KGB, a business complex, and the mafia."[4]

To date, these characterizations have not been grounded in any solid, empirical framework. This study did not begin with prior assumptions about the monolithic nature and immutability of the IRGC's domestic power. Instead, this monograph assesses the extent of the IRGC's penetration into Iran's society, economy, and political landscape; it frames the IRGC as an ultimately multidimensional

---

[2]  Gharargah-e Sazandegiye Khatam al-Anbia (Ghorb), homepage, February 20, 2007.

[3]  Comments by an Iranian-born scholar at a RAND-sponsored conference, Rome, Italy, October 29, 2007.

[4]  Quoted in Greg Bruno, "Backgrounder: The Islamic Revolutionary Guards Corps (IRGC)," Council on Foreign Relations, October 25, 2007.

institution that is certainly capable of provoking dissent and opposition through its oligarchic tendencies and domination of key economic sectors but that has built networks of constituents as well, co-opting various segments of the Iranian populace into its orbit via indoctrination or more tangible expressions of financial patronage.[5] By offering a comprehensive examination of the IRGC's domestic levers, we aim to illuminate the ways in which it portrays itself to the Iranian populace and the ways in which its future will be shaped by forces that it may or may not control.

One outcome of this analysis is the conclusion that the IRGC's omnipresence in Iran does not necessarily guarantee its omnipotence. Both internal and external threats to the organization's future remain present and viable, with factionalism being a particular concern. As one actor among many within Iran's factionalized political system, the IRGC's leadership, rank and file, and veterans are not immune to the debates over pragmatism and dogmatism that characterize the broader political spectrum.[6] Therefore, another challenge to the IRGC is the dilution of its corporate cohesion—as it delves more and more deeply into business ventures, there is a risk that corruption and economic self-interest may erode its professionalism and military capabilities. In this respect, the rise of the Pasdaran may be usefully compared to the trajectory of the Chinese People's Liberation Army (PLA) in the early and mid-1990s, raising further questions about the supposed uniqueness of the IRGC within the international system.

To fully illuminate these issues, this study shifted the methodology employed by previous studies, which have tended toward threat

---

[5]  In this respect, our study built on and drew from a previous RAND report on the Iranian military and IRGC as domestic political actors: Nikola B. Schahgaldian and Gina Barkhordarian, *The Iranian Military Under the Islamic Republic*, Santa Monica, Calif.: RAND Corporation, R-3473-USDP, 1987. For another look at the IRGC as a domestic political actor, see Kenneth R. Katzman, "The Pasdaran: Institutionalization of Revolutionary Armed Force," *Iranian Studies*, Vol. 26, No. 3–4, Summer 1993, pp. 389–402; and Kenneth Katzman, *The Warriors of Islam: Iran's Revolutionary Guards*, Boulder, Colo.: Westview Press, 1993.

[6]  Alireza Alavitabar, "Nezamian and gozar be Democracy" (The military and the path toward democracy), Web page, 2005.

assessments of the IRGC as a more traditional military organization.[7] In this monograph, we treat the IRGC as a deeply entrenched socio-political-economic entity that has both influenced and been influenced by the larger trajectory of the Islamic Republic of Iran. To do this, we draw from sources not normally incorporated in similar Western research, particularly indigenous Persian-language material, often from the IRGC's own media outlets and those of its companies, and field insights of scholars with access to Iranians from a broad societal and geographic spectrum. We also pay particular attention to the historical precedents for each of the IRGC's various internal roles, showing their origins and ebb and flow through the Islamic Republic's development. This historical inquiry is not simply background. Within the factional debates that characterize Iran's political landscape, the IRGC leadership appears to believe that its legitimacy is dependent on reviving and burnishing its role in the foundational myths of the Islamic Republic of Iran—the suppression of internal enemies during the revolution's early days, a role in the "sacred defense" during the Iran-Iraq War, and the postwar economic reconstruction. The latter has become particularly important as a current justification for the IRGC's deepening involvement in Iran's business sectors. For their part, domestic opponents of the IRGC's ascendancy have also attempted to revise the story of the institution's role in the Islamic Republic's early history.[8]

With these dynamics in mind, this monograph is structured as follows:

---

[7]  For important studies on the IRGC's military missions and capabilities, see Anthony H. Cordesman, *Iran's Developing Military Capabilities*, Washington D.C.: Center for Strategic and International Studies, 2005, and Michael Eisenstadt, "The Armed Forces of the Islamic Republic of Iran," *Middle East Review of International Affairs*, Vol. 5, No. 1, March 2001, pp. 13–30.

[8]  The best example of this appeared in October 2007, when Chairman of the Assembly of Experts Ali Akbar Rafsanjani disclosed the existence of a previously secret correspondence between IRGC commander Mohsen Rezai and Khomeini in 1988, in which Rezai advised that the Iran-Iraq War could not be won. With this letter, Rafsanjani effectively neutralized timeworn accusations by the IRGC that he alone was the sole proponent of the Iran-Iraq ceasefire and burnished his nationalist credentials while tempering those of the Guards. See Rasool Nafisi, "The Khomeini Letter: Is Rafsanjani Warning the Hardliners?" Iranian.com, October 11, 2006.

- Chapter Two situates the IRGC within the context of Iran's larger security bureaucracy and factional landscape, showing how internal competition, both formal and informal, has impacted the evolution of the IRGC and defining what is meant by ideological groupings, such as "reformist" and "conservative."
- In Chapter Three, we cover the origins and development of the IRGC's internal roles, exploring how the organization consolidated its control and expanded its domestic presence in the contentious postrevolutionary period and during the Iran-Iraq War. We also highlight the impetus behind the formation of its paramilitary "peoples' militia," the Basij Resistance Force, and the significance of that group's recent formal merger with the IRGC.
- Having set this foundation, Chapter Four canvases the IRGC's broad ideological outreach to the Iranian populace—its indoctrination, training, and media activities—which are intended to bolster loyalty to the regime, inculcate future and current members with a shared identity, and perhaps distract from the Pasdaran's corruption and monopolization of key economic sectors. Although it is difficult to discern the populace's receptivity to this ideological activism, we argue that any cynicism and resentment may be balanced by the financial benefits and promises of social mobility offered by IRGC training, which are likely appealing to certain marginalized population segments.
- Chapter Five examines the IRGC's economic and commercial activities. It is here that the institution's multidimensional nature becomes most apparent—the Pasdaran's expansion into the business realm has the potential to both displace and co-opt traditional financial elites. Similarly, its economic nepotism is accompanied by a broad range of public works initiatives in the rural periphery that have indisputably improved the economies of these regions.
- Chapter Six treats the IRGC as a political actor, arguing that, given its indoctrination efforts and economic presence, the IRGC is well positioned to become Iran's preeminent political force. Yet whether or not it currently functions as an effective counter-authority to the Supreme Leader is uncertain; the IRGC's power

is ultimately circumscribed by the system of checks and balances inherent in the Iranian political system, as well as factional disputes that both surround and permeate the institution and its network of veterans. This chapter covers instances in which these factional differences have risen to the surface and, based on this, postulates potential scenarios for the IRGC's future.

- Chapter Seven summarizes our conclusions and offers a research agenda for a deeper understanding of the Pasdaran that draws on initial comparative insights from the trajectories of the Pakistani military and Chinese PLA, which have also functioned as powerful and expansive political-economic actors but have evolved in different and unexpected ways.
- Five appendixes present additional background on IRGC-affiliated companies (Appendix A), background on key IRGC personnel (active and former; Appendix B), a timeline comparing key events in the development of the Islamic Republic with the evolution of the IRGC (Appendix C), a map of Iran (Appendix D), and a glossary of Persian terms (Appendix E).

# CHAPTER TWO

# The IRGC in Context: Iran's Security and Political Landscape

Before exploring the IRGC's varied domestic roles, it is first necessary to situate it within the larger framework of Iran's security bureaucracy and political landscape. Setting this context is important for two reasons. First, the IRGC operates within a system that is highly factionalized along both informal and formal lines. Despite its dominance, the IRGC by no means has a total monopoly on internal security or military force, and it frequently vies with other institutions for visibility, power, and resources. This rivalry often sheds light on IRGC actions that may appear at first glance to be detrimental to the larger interests of the state.

In many cases, these other security organs are staffed by ex-IRGC officers. Yet it does not follow automatically that these individuals continue to act in lockstep with the corporate interests of the IRGC— office-holding tends to generate its own specific set of imperatives and priorities that can challenge or even completely offset the powerful social bonds created by shared war experiences or military indoctrination. A good example is ex-IRGC Brigadier General Mohammad Baqer Qalibaf, who, while serving as the commander of the Law Enforcement Forces (LEF) during the latter half of the Khatami administration, clamped down on the street violence of the hardline vigilante group Ansar-e Hezbollah—itself loosely linked to the Basij and IRGC veterans—in apparent support for the reformists' cause.

The system's ideological factionalism has also permeated the IRGC. Certainly, current and former Pasdaran are bound by a corporate outlook that is broadly opportunistic, authoritarian, and populist. Yet they are also susceptible to the same debates and dilemmas that dominate Iranian political life: balancing dogmatism and pragmatism, reconciling modernity with fidelity to the revolution's ideals, and integrating economic progress with cultural authenticity. Exploring where Iran's various ideological factions stand on these issues and defining what exactly is meant by "reformist" or "conservative" are critical to discerning future trajectories for the IRGC.

## The IRGC in Iran's Security Hierarchy

As a military institution, the IRGC has an estimated 120,000 serving personnel who fulfill a number of functions related to internal security, external defense, and regime survival, and it fields an army, air force, and navy. Reflecting its original charter of defending the revolution, there are IRGC installations in all of Iran's major cities, organized into quick-reaction groups that serve as a reserve against unrest. Aside from urban areas, the IRGC operates in rural regions with other security forces in missions that include border control, counternarcotics, and disaster relief. The IRGC has primacy over Iranian unconventional warfare options, it maintains tight control over the development and deployment of Iran's ballistic missiles, and it wields an external terrorism capability through its elite Qods Force.[1] Were Iran to develop and field nuclear weapons, oversight of their storage, training, and deployment infrastructure would likely fall to the IRGC.

Within Iran's defense and security establishment, a complex web of bureaucracy regulates the IRGC's authority and power—at least on paper. These formal structures were originally intended to foster interservice coordination with the regular military, or Artesh, mitigating the severe problems of battlefield coordination that arose between the regular forces and the IRGC during the latter stages of the Iran-Iraq War. In 1988, the regime created the Joint Armed Forces General Staff, which brought together the leading officers from the regular army and

---

[1]    Cordesman (2005, pp. 45–48).

the IRGC. In addition, postwar reforms—such as the 1989 creation of the Ministry of Defense and Armed Forces Logistics—helped reduce the autonomy of the IRGC. Today, the IRGC is under an integrated command with Iran's professional armed forces at the General Staff level.

Parallel to this military chain of command, major national security issues are decided in the Supreme National Security Council (SNSC), which includes the president, the defense and foreign ministers, the commander of the Revolutionary Guards, and several appointees or "representatives" of the Supreme Leader (see Figure 2.1). This council is broadly reflective of the elite. Secretary of the SNSC Saeed Jalili, who replaced Ali Larijani in October 2007, is roughly the equivalent of the U.S. National Security Adviser. Within this structure, it is important to observe above all else that current President Ahmadine-

**Figure 2.1**
**Iran's National Security Establishment**

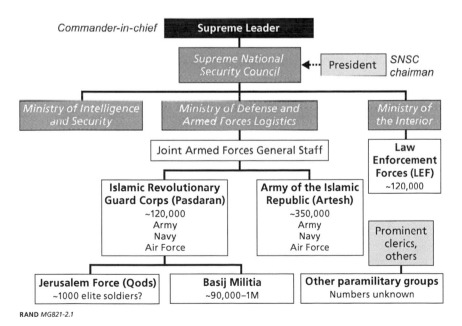

jad, despite his chairmanship of the SNSC and his headline-grabbing bravado, actually wields little authority over matters of defense. It is the Supreme Leader—currently Ayatollah Ali Khamenei—who wields constitutional authority as commander-in-chief and, perhaps more importantly, exercises vast influence through his mediating role, personal relationships with top commanders, and the presence of his clerical representatives throughout the security institutions. In addition, individuals appear to matter more than institutions when considering national security decisionmaking. The Supreme Leader has special representatives in the SNSC (Rowhani and Larijani) and special advisers, such as former Foreign Minister Akbar Velayati and former IRGC commander in chief Rahim Safavi, on his Strategic Council for Foreign Relations. All of these former officials and others are likely to be consulted by him when they do not participate in important sessions of the SNSC.

There are two other security agencies with which the IRGC both cooperates and competes: the Ministry of Intelligence and Security (MOIS) and the LEF. Comprising an estimated 30,000 personnel, the MOIS is responsible under the constitution for both foreign intelligence collection and domestic countersubversion. Prior to 1999, the organization was widely feared for its assassination of dissident activists abroad and in Iran. During the presidency of Mohammad Khatami, however, the MOIS was purged of many hardliners and has largely abandoned its policy of assassination.[2] Overseas, the MOIS reportedly liaises with several foreign Shi'a militant groups and insurgent organizations. These relationships probably bring the MOIS into competition with the Qods Force.[3]

Subordinate to the Ministry of the Interior, the LEF is Iran's national gendarmerie and includes roughly 120,000 personnel. This institution's diverse responsibilities include counternarcotics, riot control, border protection, morals enforcement, and anticorruption. In the event of an attack on the homeland, the LEF could be expected to aug-

---

[2]   Wilfried Buchta, "Iran's Security Sector: An Overview," paper presented at Challenges to Security Sector Governance in the Middle East, Geneva, July 12, 2004, pp. 13–16.

[3]   Radio Free Europe/Radio Liberty, *RFE/RL Iran Report*, Vol. 8, No. 31, August 9, 2005a.

ment IRGC and Basij paramilitaries, adding marginal capability as a light mechanized force. It is unclear, however, if Tehran's defense doctrine has incorporated the LEF into this role.

The LEF has been widely criticized for its inefficiency and poor discipline, including its facilitation of vigilante attacks on student demonstrators during the 1999 riots. Yet after the June 2000 appointment of Mohammad Baqer Qalibaf, a former IRGC Air Force commander, as its new chief, the force gradually improved its equipment inventory, policing capability, and professionalism.[4] And, as noted earlier, Qalibaf brought the force into occasional conflict with the ultraconservative "pressure groups."[5]

It is important to note that Figure 2.1, which portrays the IRGC as submerged beneath a web of oversight and coordinating bodies and as seemingly co-equal to the MOIS, LEF, and regular forces, is an inadequate representation of its true political influence. This is primarily due to the importance of informal power networks and a process of negotiation and consensus among competing factions in Iranian decisionmaking. These networks transcend, and in some cases supplant, the official bureaucratic structures—and much of their relative power may reside in their access and proximity to the Supreme Leader. As noted by scholar William Samii, Iran's factional landscape

> cannot easily be understood through a systems or organizational approach. Individuals in and out of government are connected through kinship, marriage, and place of origin. An individual's service branch during the Iran-Iraq War (e.g. IRGC, Basij, Army

---

[4] See the editorial in a reformist daily praising the LEF for its conduct during student protests and for confronting Ansar-e Hezbollah members: *Towse'eh* (Persian), "Iran: Report Views Positive Change of LEF Towards Students," FBIS IAP20030627000013, June 16, 2003.

[5] A. William Samii, "Factionalism in Iran's Domestic Security Forces," *Middle East Intelligence Bulletin*, Vol. 4, No. 2, February 2002. On June 10, 2003, for example, the LEF arrested the head of the Ansar-e Hezbollah and three other members in Mashhad. Radio Free Europe/Radio Liberty, *RFE/RL Iran Report*, Vol. 6, No. 25, June 16, 2003; see also, *Yas-e Now* (Persian) "Iran: Political Figures Comment on Violent Groups, Elections, Other Issues," FBIS IAP2003121600005, December 8, 2005.

ground forces) and education, whether in a seminary or a military academy, also affect the connections he is likely to have.[6]

Taking these dynamics into account, we argue that much of the IRGC's domestic ascendancy has been encouraged by the inherently complex structure of the Iranian political system. Because this system has built-in redundancy and multiple centers of power, and because it relies on a ponderous process of checks and balances among different organizations, there is a default drift toward "behind-the-scenes" bargaining and informal networking.

Thus, when we refer to the IRGC in this monograph, we mean not only the formal institution of active military personnel but also the networks of IRGC veterans and former members whose ascension has been facilitated by the informality of Iranian political life. Such influential figures as Ali Larijani (until recently, secretary of the SNSC), Ezzatolah Zarghami (head of the Islamic Republic of Iran Broadcasting), Mohsen Rezai (secretary of the Expediency Council), and assorted heads of economic foundations, or *bonyads*, are all part of the IRGC's networks. And behind these personal networks lie robust intellectual resources: two IRGC-run universities, two think tanks, and assorted policy journals and media outlets.

Many analyses and commentaries have imparted a certain ideological homogeneity to these networks and the IRGC writ large that can best be described as authoritarian, populist, and, in some cases, anticlerical. Much of this may stem from the similar age cohort of many members, which has often been termed the "war generation"— referring to the searing, formative experience of the Iran-Iraq War. Certainly, this experience shaped political outlooks and forged enduring social bonds among individuals who fought in the same battle or served under the same commander. At least one Iranian scholar asserted to a RAND researcher in 2005 that, with the election of Ahmadinejad and the insertion of his ex-IRGC coterie into key positions of power,

---

[6]  Samii (2002).

this shared outlook would be strong enough to "mitigate the fractious policy infighting that defined the Khatami era."[7]

As our analysis reveals throughout this report, this has not been the case. Ahmadinejad's tenure—and even his electoral campaign itself—has not gone unchallenged by the IRGC. Factionalism remains a feature of the Iranian system and, as we argue in this monograph, could become an increasing challenge to the IRGC itself. Moreover, like any elite organization, the IRGC's corporate identity has not been able to completely and irrevocably subsume the attachments of locale, class, familial ties, ethnicity, or sect among its members. As we discuss in Chapter Five, these unofficial identities have surfaced at key junctures in the evolution of the IRGC and the trajectory of the Islamic Republic of Iran. The removal or ascendancy of a key figure, an instance of internal unrest, an election, or a critical policy debate have provoked dissent and will continue to do so.

As the network of guards and ex-guards continues to expand and diversify its domestic roles, particularly on economic matters, the IRGC's ability to resolve these internal tensions may become further jeopardized. Arguably, its membership will become responsive to a widening set of constituencies and interests that may bear little resemblance to the original, foundational values of an elite military organization.[8]

## Iran's Factional Landscape

To better illuminate these current and potential fissures, discussed later in this monograph, it is helpful to first situate the IRGC within the factional landscape of Iranian politics. It is difficult to neatly label individuals, factions, or parties in the Iranian system as reformist or conservative. Any useful categorizations are often quite elastic and divide

---

[7] Authors' telephone conversation with a Tehran-based political scientist, December 12, 2005.

[8] It is regarding these dynamics that we see great value in a comparative approach that draws from studies of the PLA and the Pakistani military.

further, often depending on the specific issue in question. Moreover, the factions often divide into subgroups, depending on the domestic or foreign policy issue. Understanding how these groups interact and the stakes in their rivalry is important in assessing the IRGC's political future. Instead of acting as a unified factional force itself, the IRGC can be better conceived as an institution over which the various ideological factions may compete for control and influence. This is consistent with the broader processes at work in the Islamic Republic of Iran. As noted by one observer,

> Rather than serve as an autonomous regulator and arbiter of (rivalries), the state is the principal arena in which the competition takes place. Rival claims over parts of the state and its resources are constantly played out, at times with considerable acrimony.[9]

Taking these dynamics into account, we have adopted the following broad typology that draws from a 2008 RAND study and is based on the insights of a scholar with extensive field experience in the Islamic Republic.[10] These rough fissures began to surface soon after the success of the revolution but arguably reached their full apogee at the end of the Iran-Iraq War and, especially, during the administra-

---

[9]   International Crisis Group, "Iran: Ahmadi-Nejad's Tumultuous Presidency," International Crisis Group, *Middle East Briefing*, No. 21, Tehran and Brussels, February 6, 2007, p. 2.

[10]   Jerrold D. Green, Frederic Wehrey, and Charles Wolf, Jr., *Understanding Iran*, Santa Monica, Calif.: RAND Corporation, MG-771-SRF, 2008. Our typology also draws from Mehran Kamrava, "Iranian National-Security Debates: Factionalism and Lost Opportunities," Middle East Policy, Vol. 14, No. 2, Summer 2007, pp. 84–100, and Wilfried Buchta, *Who Rules Iran? The Structure of Power in the Islamic Republic*, Washington, D.C.: Washington Institute for Near East Policy and the Konrad Adenauer Stiftung, 2000, pp. 11–21. We have also drawn from Iranian sources on political factionalism: Hossein Bashiriyeh, *Dibachei bar jamee shenasiy-e Iran* (An introduction to the sociology of politics in Iran), 2nd ed., Tehran: Nashr-e Negah-e Moaser Publications, 2002; Said Hajjarian, *Jomhuriyat: Afsunzodai az Ghodrat* (Republicanism: Rubbing off charm from power), 2nd ed., Tehran: Tarh-e No Publications, 2000; Sadegh Zibakalam, *Veda ba dovvom-e Khordad* (Farewell with 2nd of Khordad), 1st ed., Tehran: Rouzane Publications, 2003; Mohammad Ghouchani, "Etelafhaye rangi: Moghadamei bar etelafhaye siasi dar Iran" (Colorful coalitions: An introduction to the political coalitions in Iran), *Nameh*, No. 50, May 2006.

tion of President Mohammad Khatami (1997–2005), whose efforts to promote a more open political culture had the unintended effect of encouraging elite factionalism.

- *Conservative Traditionalists.* This current can be best described as the main and largest faction, advocating a patriarchal Islamic government, consolidation of the revolution's gains, preservation of a traditional lifestyle, promotion of self-sufficiency with no dependence on the outside world, and cultural purity. Among its constituents, this trend counts the lower-middle classes, lower-ranking clerics, and *bazaari* merchants (some bazaaris also support other factions, such as the reformists). Its reach extends into nearly all the major institutions of the state, from the Office of the Supreme Leader on down. Key formal groupings include the Association of Qom Seminary Teachers and the Association of Militant Clergy (Jameeh Rowhaniyyat-e Mobarez).

- *Reformist Cluster.* From the mid-to-late 1980s onward, the conservative trend was subjected to fissures over questions of pragmatism, doctrinal purity, and Iran's relationship with the world. From these debates emerged a group of more moderate clerics in 1988, which split from the Association of Militant Clergy and formed the Society for Militant Clerics (Majma-e Rowhaniyoun-e Mobarez). Clustered around Mehdi Karrubi and Mohammad Khatami, this trend argued for the promotion of civil society, a relaxation of political and social controls, economic openness, a cultural renaissance, and more interaction with the outside world. In this sense, they drew inspiration from a tradition of Iranian thinkers, including Ali Shariati and, later, Abdul Karim Soroush, who synthesized Islamic moral concepts with modern Enlightenment political philosophy to argue that there was no inherent tension between democracy and Islamic society. This broad clustering became ascendant in the mid-1990s, first inserting supporters into the Majles (Iran's national parliament) and then having its candidate, Mohammad Khatami, elected to the presidency in 1997. The popularity of this current was strongest among the intelligentsia, writers, and students, though it never succeeded in marshaling the approval of the Supreme Leader—a fatal flaw that facilitated the political interference of the IRGC and defeat of the reformists.

- *Pragmatic Conservatives.* Situated somewhere between the first and the second factions is a cluster of what have been termed the "pragmatic conservatives." This trend has organized itself within two parties: the Executives of Construction Party (Hezbe Kargozaran Sazandegi), which supported the reformists' approach to culture, and the Justice and Development Party (Hezbe E'tedal va Tose'eh), which leaned toward the conservative traditionalists on cultural issues. The camp as a whole was inspired by the intellectual work of a number of economic theorists who believed in economic modernization from above (the so-called "China model") and argued for increased technical and financial cooperation with the West (including the United States); but, unlike the reformists, they showed little interest in the democratization of politics. This current has often reversed its position on critical domestic issues, spurring charges of opportunism from its rivals among the conservative traditionalist and the new conservative clusters, who depict themselves quite literally and self-righteously as "principlists" who have remained steadfast to the revolution's ideals. The pragmatists have traditionally derived support from the *bazaari* merchant class, students, the urban middle classes, and technocrats.

- *Radicals.* This is the grouping that has been most closely identified with the "rise" of the IRGC as a political force, beginning with its assumption of provincial administration posts in 2003 and leading up to the election of President Mahmoud Ahmadinejad in 2005. The political group encapsulating this current was the Abadgaran-e Iran-e Islami (Developers of Islamic Iran), which was composed of IRGC and Basij war veterans. Many of them rose to mid- and senior-level positions but were subsequently marginalized during the Rafsanjani era. During the 2005 elections, the "new conservatives" appealed principally to the urban poor and provincial classes.

Although the Office of the Supreme Leader and other key institutions have generally remained squarely the purview of the conservative traditionalists, each of the other currents has also had its heyday, enjoying a period of formal political power through control of the Majles and the presidency.

- 1989–1997: Rafsanjani and the pragmatists presided over Iran's postwar reconstruction. During this period, the IRGC and ex-IRGC personnel were largely marginalized from political power.
- 1997–2005: Khatami and the reformist cluster emphasized the growth of civil society and the so-called "dialogue of civilizations." Here, the IRGC began its political ascendancy, allying with conservatives to challenge Khatami's reforms.
- 2005–present: Ahmadinejad, the radical, and the Revolutionary Guards came to power. Some have labeled this Iran's "Third Revolution."

As we discuss more fully in Chapter Seven, the "rise" of the IRGC has been met with its own set of factional debates over the very same questions of pragmatism versus dogmatism and, especially, over the economic opportunity costs inflicted by Iran's isolation and the stridency of the Ahmadinejad presidency. These factional currents continue to permeate and shape the diverse domestic roles of the IRGC, whose origins and evolution are discussed in the next chapter.

# CHAPTER THREE

# The IRGC's Diverse Domestic Roles: Origins and Evolution

The IRGC's expansive reach into Iran's economy, politics, and society has far exceeded its original, rather modest mandate. Understanding the degree of this divergence from its formal charter and, especially, from the vision outlined for it by Ayatollah Khomeini is critical to understanding how it is received by the Iranian public and by Iran's ideological factions. In attempting to curry legitimacy with various segments of the Iranian populace, the IRGC frequently marshals the authority of Ayatollah Khomeini as well as its role in reconstructing the country after the "imposed war" or the "sacred defense," i.e., the Iran-Iraq War.

Speaking to the Islamic Republic of Iran News Agency (IRNA) in August 2007, then IRGC commander Major General Rahim Safavi argued that, since the termination of the Iran-Iraq War,

> the IRGC has assumed three major and two peripheral missions. The major missions of the IRGC involve defense, security, and cultural issues and its peripheral missions are related to the construction of the country and carrying out relief and rescue operations during natural disasters.[1]

While grounding its current missions in the revolutionary and postwar past, the IRGC is also careful to present itself as continually

---

[1] IRNA, "Iran: Guards Commander Says Change in Guards Strategy Necessary," FBIS IAP20070817950094, August 17, 2007c.

adapting to new strategic circumstances. This is especially true regarding what Safavi termed the recent intensification of a "cultural war" being waged by the United States against the Iranian populace. To mobilize the population against this perceived challenge, the IRGC has expanded its ideological, training, and education roles. According to Safavi,

> The IRGC does not intervene in the cultural activities of other government organizations and bodies. However, based on the nature of the IRGC, which is intertwined with belief and military activities, the organization's orientation is to enhance the forces' Islamic and ideological beliefs; and this is a part of the duties vested with the IRGC.[2]

Of course, the hidden subtext of this "cultural defense" is the IRGC's interest in bolstering its own institutional credibility and shoring up the revolution's sagging appeal in the eyes of the populace. The IRGC's commanders and ideologues appear to perceive that much of this effort is contingent on aligning their institution's current activities with the original intent and vision of the Islamic Republic's founders.

## Postrevolutionary Developments: Consolidating Internal Control

The IRGC was originally conceptualized by its founders as a popular militia force to monitor the remainders of the shah's military and protect the state from possible counterrevolutionary activity. On May 5, 1979, roughly one month after declaring the Islamic Republic, Ayatollah Khomeini issued a decree ordering the Revolutionary Council to establish the Sepah-e Pasdaran-e Enghelab-e Islami (literally, Army of the Guardians of the Islamic Revolution).[3] This new force differed from

---

[2]   IRNA (2007c).

[3]   The idea of creating a parallel military structure enriched by and imbued with Islamic ideology in fact preceded the 1979 revolution. While still in exile in Paris, some of the members of the Freedom Movement, a moderate political group opposed to the shah, introduced

the shah's imperial army in its mission in that it accorded primacy to an *internal* role against potential counterrevolutionaries while at the same time pushing for the export of the revolution. The Revolutionary Council enumerated the duties of the IRGC in eight categories:[4]

- assisting police and security forces in the apprehension or liquidation of counterrevolutionary elements
- battling armed counterrevolutionaries
- defending against attacks and the activities of foreign forces *inside* the country
- coordinating and cooperating with the country's armed forces
- training subordinate IRGC personnel in moral, ideological, and politico-military matters
- assisting the Islamic Republic in the implementation of the Islamic Revolution
- supporting liberation movements and their call for justice of the oppressed people of the world under the tutelage of the leader of the Revolution of the Islamic Republic
- utilizing the human resources and expertise of the IRGC to deal with national calamities and unexpected catastrophes and supporting the developmental plans of the Islamic Republic to completely maximize the IRGC's resources.

The IRGC's domestic roles were further delineated in the Islamic Republic of Iran's constitution, ratified on November 15, 1979. Article 150 of the document defines the role and functions of the IRGC:

> The Islamic Revolutionary Guards Corps, organized in the early days of the triumph of the Revolution, is to be maintained so that it may continue in its role of guarding the Revolution and

---

the idea of creating a revolutionary army much like that of Algeria's freedom fighters. The idea originated with Ayatollah Khomeini and, after his approval, the early founders of what was to become the IRGC started to accept volunteers who were eventually sent to Syria and Lebanon for military training.

[4]    Petrochemical Research and Technology Company, Event List, Web page, October 7, 1997.

its achievements. The scope of duties of the Corps, and its areas of responsibility, in relation to the duties and areas of responsibility of the other armed forces, are to be determined by law, with emphasis on brotherly cooperation and harmony among them.[5]

Article 151 seems to augur the formation of the Basij and indicates its formal mission:

The government is oblige[d] to provide a program of military training, with all requisite facilities, for all its citizens, in accordance with the Islamic criteria, in such a way that all citizens will always be able to engage in the armed defense of the Islamic Republic of Iran. The possession of arms, however, requires the granting of permission by the competent authorities.[6]

It is important to note, however, that despite the constitutional primacy accorded to it by the revolution, the IRGC's domestic ascendancy over other security institutions was not preordained. In the chaotic aftermath of the Islamic Revolution, the IRGC was just one of several security instruments used by the leaders of the new state against existential threats and, at times, wildly exaggerated challenges posed by an array of armed groups—both leftists (the communist Tudeh party and the Marxist Mujahideen-e Khalq [MEK]), ethnic insurgents such as the Kurds, and monarchists.[7] The IRGC generally operated outside of the sphere and jurisdiction of the regular police and army forces controlled by the short-lived provisional government headed by Prime Minister Mehdi Bazargan. The new government's security organs worked to extirpate the leftists but were far less effective in this task than were the Islamist paramilitary organizations, whose proficiency

---

[5]   "Constitution of the Islamic Republic of Iran," English translation, Iranian Embassy, Ottawa, Canada, 1979.

[6]   "Constitution of the Islamic Republic of Iran" (1979).

[7]   See various publications by opposition groups, such as "Rah e Azadi" and "Mojahed." See also Kenneth M. Pollack, *The Persian Puzzle: The Conflict Between Iran and America*, New York: Random House, 2004, pp. 149–150.

in street violence and the forcible silencing of dissent were to become enduring features of Iranian political life.

In the realm of Islamist paramilitary groups, the IRGC was not without its fair share of competitors in enforcing revolutionary ideals, particularly from the *komitehs* (committees). These were freelance bands of local Islamists who arrogated to themselves the power of justice and administration over assorted neighborhoods in major cities throughout the Islamic Republic.[8] Roughly 1,000 *komitehs* operated in Tehran alone in the months after the fall of the shah, arbitrarily arresting anyone they deemed a threat to the republic's new sociopolitical order. Although the *komitehs* and the IRGC often drew from the same pool of volunteers, there was often friction between them.

Another variant of these local-level organizations were the "revolutionary tribunals" that operated de facto courts across the country. These virtual "kangaroo courts" tried and summarily executed thousands of people who were suspected of counterrevolutionary crimes. Finally, the pro-Khomeini Islamic Republic Party (IRP), which was the home of the most doctrinaire Islamist figures in Iran, may have had its own paramilitary groups as it waged a struggle to indoctrinate the country and the provisional government.

The triumph of the IRGC over these other groups was ultimately achieved by demonstrating its superior effectiveness as a guard for the nascent revolutionary regime during the Iran-Iraq War.

## The Sacred Defense: The IRGC in the Iran-Iraq War

As the new regime fought for its survival, the IRGC was the principal institution responsible for suppressing uprisings by separatist Kurds, Baluchs, and Turkmen, as well as confronting the MEK after it openly broke with Khomeini in June 1981.[9] Yet despite these successes, it never completely achieved a monopoly over the regime's internal policing functions. Indeed, the fractious rivalry among the informal paramili-

---

8    Pollack (2004, p. 150).

9    Buchta (2000, p. 67).

taries that marked the revolution's early days has, in a sense, been institutionalized into a domestic security establishment that is characterized by parallelism, redundancy, and competition for resources.

Today, the IRGC attempts to strengthen its legitimacy by emphasizing its role in the "sacred defense" of the Islamic Republic against Iraq and, simultaneously, challenges originating from inside the country. This theme informs much of its larger societal, economic, and political outreach, as discussed later on in this monograph. For example, much of its construction and public-works activities are framed as a sort of reenactment or a continuation of its vaunted role in the aftermath of the Iran-Iraq War. Of course, whether or not this actually resonates with Iranian society remains an open question. As one Iranian-born scholar and frequent visitor to the Islamic Republic has observed:

> The bravery of the IRGC (during the Iran-Iraq War) is mostly an idea propagated by the government with no particular appeal or currency within Iran itself. In fact, many Iranians blame the IRGC for an excessively long and futile eight-year war against Iraq. Many believe that Iran, with a population two times larger than that of Iraq, could not defeat its forces because of the Guards' nadanam kari (inexperience), emotionality, and ideological zealotry.[10]

However, the above statement may not apply to a significant portions of Iran's population. Iranians whose sons and husbands became *shahids*, or martyrs, may view the IRGC more reverentially. These Iranians tend to be supportive of the Islamic Republic and the IRGC as political institutions.

What has not been widely recognized outside of Iran is the fact that many, if not most, IRGC commanders, along with revolutionary leaders such as Khomeini, viewed the war not just as a struggle for the territorial integrity of the Iranian state but instead as an opportunity to further consolidate and institutionalize the revolution, purging it

---

[10] Authors' correspondence with an Iranian-born scholar, October 24, 2007.

of known and potential opponents.[11] Arguably, this prerogative some-
times took precedence over matters of strategy and military expediency. This is perhaps demonstrated by the IRGC's efforts to politically
marginalize the regular army by prolonging the war. As long as the regular army was stretched thin and fully deployed on the western border,
it could not mount any sort of a coup d'etat against Khomeini and his
cohorts. This was not an inconsequential concern for the IRGC leaders
and their IRP patrons, as the professional army had mounted several
coup attempts in the summer of 1980 just before the Iraqi invasion.

Thus, the immediate postrevolutionary period and the Iran-Iraq
War revealed several important themes that continue to define the
development of the IRGC's domestic roles: competition with other
security institutions, the tension between ideological doctrine and
strategic expediency, and the consolidation of domestic institutional
control by mobilizing for external defense. On this latter imperative,
the IRGC's leadership has relied extensively on the Basij Resistance
Forces, its paramilitary affiliate of lightly armed, often poorly trained
auxiliaries whose command structure was formally merged with that
of the IRGC in 2007.[12] More than any other IRGC entity, the Basij
has evolved to become the institution's most visible, omnipresent face
to the Iranian population and has seen its domestic functions expand
significantly since its early role in the Iran-Iraq War.

## "Popularizing" the IRGC: The Development of the Basij Resistance Force

Many revolutionary regimes have relied on "popular militias" or a
"people's army," in which sheer numbers and ideological fervor are
believed to compensate for a deficit in military competence and equipment. In many cases, these organizations' military role is subordinated

---

[11]   Ervand Abrahamian, *The Iranian Mojahedin*, New Haven, Conn: Yale University Press,
1992, pp. 63–64, 259.

[12]   Mehr News Agency "IRGC Commander Takes Charge of Basij Forces," September 29,
2007.

to their function of indoctrinating the populace and suppressing internal dissent.

Formed less than a year after the IRGC, the Basij's early development certainly seemed to embody these features—when Ayatollah Khomeini directed its creation, he appealed for a "20 million–man militia" to defend the republic from both *external* aggression from the United States and from the revolution's *internal* enemies.[13] As in the case of the IRGC, the formation of the Basij was at least partially a response to the revolutionary competition that defined the political scene after the fall of the Bazargan government on November 11, 1979. Leftist organizations aligned with Khomeini had pressed for some sort of "popular" force that, once created, would allow for the disbandment of the ex-shah's forces. As noted earlier, many of these leftist groups already had their own armed wings, hence the strong impetus for a broad-based Islamist people's militia.[14]

At a gathering of Basij members in 2006, Basij commander Hussein Hamadani summarized the early history of the Basij, or at least the IRGC's version of it, enumerating its services to the revolution as follows:

- The Basij maintained security in the absence of an effective police force in the early years of the revolution.
- It purged government offices of antirevolutionary elements and old-regime loyalists.
- It formed a network of information gathering on the opposition. This network was nicknamed "the 36 million [member] information network."
- It suppressed a communist uprising in the northern Caspian city of Amol and protected oil pipelines from terrorist activities in the

---

[13]  The original name of the Basij was Sazman Basij Melli, or the National Mobilization Organization. It was changed a decade later to Vahed-e Basij Mostaza'feen, or Mobilization of the Oppressed Unit, and eventually to Sazman-e Moghavemat-e Basij, or the National Resistance Mobilization.

[14]  Schahgaldian and Barkhordarian (1987, p. 88).

south. The Kurdistan uprising in the city of Paveh also was suppressed by the Basij forces.

- In the July 1980 Nojeh coup attempt by former members of the
shah's forces, a Basij member was planted inside the conspirators'
group and kept the revolutionary regime informed of the activities of the counterrevolutionaries. Afterward, he was martyred.
- For the first year of the war against Iraq, the Basij was not allowed
to interfere because of its lack of expertise; however, when it was
allowed to enter the war, the defensive position of Iran turned
into an offensive one.[15]

Battlefield conditions in the Iran-Iraq War and early political
turmoil inside Iran aided the domestic ascendancy of the Basij. Con-
fronted with the Iraqi army's static armor defenses and minefields, and
bereft of substantial mechanized forces, Iranian commanders came to
initially rely on human-wave assaults as a highly effective countermea-
sure. Many of these offensives were conducted by Basij units, composed of young boys recruited from mosques in poor neighborhoods
and, in some cases, forcibly conscripted from schools. Instilled with
religious and nationalist fervor, the Basij militia became a formidable
challenge to Iraq's more traditional and disciplined military.[16] These
early successes were important as a vehicle for the IRGC to bolster
its legitimacy in the "sacred defense," particularly vis-à-vis the regular
forces. Moreover, the early reliance on superior morale, sheer numbers, indoctrination, and youth, necessitated by Iran's conventional
military weaknesses, set the template for the Islamic Republic's current
"asymmetric" strategy of homeland defense—the conduct of partisan
warfare, defense-in-depth, and scorched-earth tactics by lightly armed
popular forces against a militarily superior opponent.

While the actual battlefield validity of this concept is open to
debate, it does afford the IRGC a useful pretext for conducting wide-

---

[15]  *Yaletharat*, Vol. 402, November 29, 2006.

[16]  Shaul Bakhash, *The Reign of the Ayatollahs: Iran and the Islamic Revolution*, New York:
Basic Books, 1984, pp. 63, 118–119; Dilip Hiro, *The Longest War: The Iran-Iraq Military
Conflict*, New York: Routledge, 1991.

spread indoctrination and training of the populace using the Basij Resistance Force as a vehicle. According to Iran's Mo'in (Auxiliary) Defense Plan, local Basij units, under the supervision of IRGC commanders, would play a prominent role in training and mobilizing the Iranian population for countrywide partisan warfare.[17] For this strategy to be effective, however, the populace must be receptive to Basij guidance and direction—hence the intensive focus on cultivating a favorable popular image of the Basij and the IRGC writ large via media outreach and by highlighting its public-works projects in the rural periphery.

Today, the Basij are present in virtually all sectors of Iranian society; there are specially organized Basij units for university students, local tribes, factory workers, and so forth. There is a strong ideological component to this omnipresence. As stated by a local IRGC commander in 2001,

> In the next decade, our problem will be the cultural onslaught and the Basij must block its progress . . . instead of creating military bases, our policy today is to create cultural societies.[18]

Despite these lofty intentions, however, there are some indications that the Basij—many of whom are drawn from the ranks of Iran's disaffected youth and elderly pensioners—hold cynical or ambivalent views of this ideological training. Basij training is frequently necessary for certain social benefits—loans, university scholarships, welfare subsidies, and the like. As stated by one 24-year-old member in a 2005 interview, "The only reason I stay in the Basij is for the money . . . many of my friends in the Basij are unhappy with the government."[19]

---

[17]   Vision of the Islamic Republic of Iran Network (Persian), "Iran Revolution Guards Hold 'Asymmetric Warfare' Ashura-5 Exercises," FBIS IAP IAP20040913000110, September 13, 2004; Vision of the Islamic Republic of Iran Network (Persian), "IRGC Ground Force Commander Speaks on Reorganization, Combat Plans" FBIS IAP 20050309000087, March 9, 2005.

[18]   Radio Free Europe/Radio Liberty, *RFE/RL Iran Report*, Vol. 4, No. 6, February 12, 2001.

[19]   International Crisis Group, "What Does Ahmadi-Nejad's Victory Mean?" *Middle East Briefing*, No. 18, Tehran and Brussels, August 2005, p. 6.

Compounding this reported cynicism, there appears to be a rural-urban split in public perceptions of the Basij, noted in a previous RAND study[20] and reinforced to us in 2006 by a longtime visitor to the Islamic Republic. In the provinces, the Basij present a more benign face through construction projects and disaster relief, while in urban areas, they are more apt to be seen quite negatively, quashing civil society activities, arresting dissidents, and confronting reformist student groups on campuses.[21]

Urban sentiments may be, moreover, affected by the Basij's affiliation with the "pressure groups" or hardline vigilantes, of which Ansar-e Hezbollah is the most widely known. Although not formally attached to the IRGC, it is reportedly staffed by Basij and IRGC veterans of the Iran-Iraq War. In the minds of the populace, therefore, it may be associated with the IRGC and thus have a direct impact on popular perceptions of its societal and political legitimacy.

The role of the Ansar also raises the important function of the IRGC as an internal security and domestic intelligence arm of the regime.

## The Guardians of the Revolution: The IRGC's Domestic Intelligence and Security Roles

As noted earlier, the suppression of internal dissent and domestic intelligence collection were among the IRGC's first mandated roles. Indeed, the guardian nature of the IRGC was embedded in its duties from its earliest days, when it liquidated political opponents of the revolutionary state, separatists, and other "morally corrupt" individuals. Today,

---

[20]  Schahgaldian and Barkhordarian (1987, p. 37).

[21]  At the same time, there have been instances in which Basij incompetence or inefficiency as emergency relief forces responding to natural disasters has provoked the ire of rural populations. As an example of Basij's urban enforcement role, on August 20, 2005, Tehran's deputy prosecutor took the remarkable step of deputizing Basij paramilitary units as police officers, giving them powers of arrest and other judicial functions. See, "Paramilitaries to Get Police Powers," in Radio Free Europe/Radio Liberty, *RFE/RL Iran Report*, Vol. 8, No. 34, August 29, 2005b.

the IRGC still performs these functions, though its relationship with other domestic and law enforcement entities, the LEF and the MOIS in particular, is frequently marked by a lack of coordination or even open rivalry.[22]

For many of the Islamic Republic of Iran's early years, the IRGC was responsible for both internal and external intelligence and security, which was carried out in conjunction with the prime minister's office. Relying on the remnants of the shah's deeply feared intelligence agency, the SAVAK, the IRGC successfully eliminated the terrorist Islamic group Forghan and the Communist Tudeh Party, and it was able to dismantle the vast networks of the MEK. The mobile units of the IRGC, *alghare'eh,* proved particularly effective in destroying counter-revolutionary opposition groups. Yet with the formation of the MOIS in 1983, the IRGC ceded much of its internal intelligence role.[23]

It was not until the election of reformist President Mohammad Khatami in 1997 and the years following that the IRGC actually regained its domestic surveillance responsibilities, albeit more informally and as a "shadow intelligence" agency.[24] Khatami's newly appointed Minister for Intelligence and Security, Hojatolislam Ali Younessi, began to set the MOIS on a path that was more cautiously tolerant of Khatami's reformist agenda for civil society, intellectual freedom, and political openness.[25] The net effect was that, as the MOIS was increasingly perceived by powerful conservatives—namely, the Supreme Leader—as a more reform-dominated entity, the IRGC steadily resumed many of its former internal security activities. This new conservative-dominated informal intelligence network, nicknamed "the parallel intelligence and security organization" by its critics, was modeled after the intelligence section of the IRGC's ground force.[26]

---

[22]   Samii (2002). See also Eisenstadt (2001).

[23]   Khaligh (2006b).

[24]   Khaligh (2006b).

[25]   Iranian Students News Agency, "Report on Ministry of Intelligence Press Conference." Gooya News, August 31, 2004.

[26]   Khaligh (2006b).

The balance among the various security and intelligence forces changed once again after the defeat of the reformists and the rise of the radicals under President Ahmadinejad in 2005. The MOIS regained some of its authority under Hojatolislam Gholamhussein Mohseni-Ejehi, who has since sought to "prove" his ministry's conservative bona fides through the widespread suppression of intellectual freedoms and civil society, spurred in large measure by the regime's fear that the United States is attempting to foment a "velvet revolution" (i.e., the erosion of revolutionary ideals via civil-society organizations and ethnic dissent) inside Iran.[27]

At present, the security division, or *Sazman-e Harassat,* of the IRGC functions much like a regular internal security and intelligence office.[28] It collects information on the opposition and separatists, arrests individuals, and imprisons them in sections of the Evin and other prisons controlled exclusively by the IRGC. Much of this activity may be conducted through the IRGC's Political and Ideological Directorate, probably under the direction of Hojattolislam Saeedi, the representative of the Supreme Leader, and his subordinate clerics. Supreme Leader Khamenei himself likely exerts a key role, as he is well known for his detailed attention to management issues, particularly on the day-to-day functioning of the IRGC. Supreme Leader Khamenei's office *(Daftar-e Rahbar)* is able to bypass the senior IRGC leadership and thus is able to directly supervise the security and intelligence activities of the IRGC.

---

[27] Farideh Farhi, "Iran's Security Outlook," *Middle East Report Online,* July 9, 2007. For information on the arrest of Western think-tank scholars, most notably Iranian-American Haleh Esfandiari, see Islamic Republic of Iran Network Television (Tehran), "OSC: Iranian TV Describes Detained Iranian-American Esfandiari as 'Mosad Spy,'" FBIS IAP20070512011017, May 12, 2007a. For information on the broader cultural and political crackdown, see Open Source Center, "Iran: Ahmadinezhad Government Reverses Civil Society Gains," Open Source Center Analysis, FBIS IAF20070620564001, June 20, 2007b.

[28] Khaligh (2006b).

## The Merger of Basij and IRGC: A Sign of the Regime's Growing Entrenchment

The prior section introduced the IRGC's domestic roles by way of a historical inquiry into its origins and early development. Factional rivalry with other militias early in the postrevolutionary period and, later, with other security institutions initially facilitated the IRGC's domestic involvement, particularly in the areas of intelligence and law enforcement. The very nature of the revolutionary regime, which conflated external plots with internal consolidation, meant that the IRGC would continue to act as a guardian of the revolution even as it expanded its role in Iran's external defense. Yet the waxing and waning of the IRGC's internal security role is often contingent on whether powerful conservative figures and clerics perceive that other security institutions, such as the MOIS or LEF, are under their control or have fallen to other factional actors. Perhaps more importantly, however, the degree of the IRGC's domestic interference is also a function of the regime's broader threat perception of internal subversion by the enemies of the revolution—namely, the United States.

Since the fall of Saddam Hussein in 2003, this perception has risen in a steady crescendo. Recent statements by the IRGC and other regime officials make clear their fixation on "psychological warfare" and the "cultural onslaught" of the United States, even if the fear of a direct attack has subsided. Whether through ethnic subversion or its support for civil society and academic exchanges, the United States is perceived to be steadily eroding the ideological foundations of the revolution. Of course, the utility of an external menace to keep the country on war footing and distract the populace from the regime's own administrative and economic failings has long been a feature of the Islamic Republic of Iran's official discourse—but this is largely a moot point. Whether real or exaggerated, this threat perception has had the effect of deepening and broadening the IRGC's populist and mobilizing outreach—often termed the promotion of "Basij culture"—into virtually every geographic, economic, and societal sector of Iran.

This dynamic was ultimately reflected in the formal merger of the command structure of the IRGC with the Basij—a move that was calculated to make the IRGC "more Basij-like" and to formally enshrine their respective increased domestic roles. In commenting on this merger in September 2007, the new IRGC commander, Mohammad Ali Jafari, confirmed the total participation of the IRGC in Iranian domestic life, with its principal focus on combating *internal* enemies:

> The new strategic guidelines of the IRGC have been changed by the directives of the leader of the revolution [Supreme Leader Khamenei]. The main mission of the IRGC from now on is to deal with the threats from the internal enemies. [The number-two priority of the corps] is to help the military in case of foreign threats.[29,30]

To some of the more idealistic founders of the IRGC, the shift toward a primary focus on internal intelligence and security has been an unwelcome deviation from the original goals of the institution. According to such critics as Mohsen Sazegara, the metamorphosis of the IRGC is the result of the influence of Mohammad Bagher Zolghadr (former deputy commander of the IRGC), Hojatolislam Rasti-Kashani (the personal representative of Ayatollah Khomeini to the Pasdaran), and Mohsen Rezai. Rezai was appointed as the chief of the intelligence division of the IRGC, which spread its reach into other branches of the IRGC as well as other parallel security organizations.[31]

One important result of this turn toward a domestic role in combating internal dissent has been an intensified focus on indoctrination, training, and education. This focus is the subject of the next chapter.

---

[29] Mehrnews, "Farmandehi niruye moghavemate basij be sardar Jafari mohavval shod" (The command of Basij was assigned to Jafari), October 2007.

[30] M. A. Jafari, "The main mission of the IRGC is to deal with the internal enemies," Mizan News, September 29, 2007.

[31] Mohsen Sazegara, "Sepah va seh enherof" (The IRGC and three aberrations), July 23, 2006. He adds that Mohsen Rezai proposed that the IRGC should organize new branches to deal with internal opposition; Sazegara disagreed, saying that it will generate an organization similar to the Brown Shirts organization in Nazi Germany. Rezai laughed, saying that it would not happen, because the Brown Shirts were (at least) educated!

# Militarizing Civil Society: The IRGC's Indoctrination, Training, and Media Activities

From Basij university student groups and paramilitary training to monthly bulletins and newspapers, the IRGC administers a vast network of outlets for propagating a sense of corporatism, cultivating loyalty to the regime, and burnishing its own institutional image.

What remains largely unknown, however, is the population's receptivity to this mobilization. As in the case of dissent against its economic expansion, discussed at length in the next chapter, there is scattered reporting of cynicism, exhaustion, and resistance toward the IRGC's ideological outreach. Yet given the breadth of its indoctrination efforts, as well as the fact that this indoctrination is frequently accompanied by more tangible benefits, such as scholarships, loans, technical job training, and societal mobility via officer commissions, it is logical to presume that the IRGC has been at least partially successful in broadening its range of constituents and supporters. The most profitable approach, therefore, is to survey the range of its ideological activism, noting potential beneficiaries and instances of support or dissent.

## The IRGC's Ideological Activism: Origins and Development

The IRGC's function of ideological outreach is not new; one of its clear responsibilities at its inception was self-indoctrination, e.g., "training

the Sepah (Revolutionary Guards) in moral, ideological, and politico-military matters."[1] To inculcate emerging elite cadres with a new
Islamic ideology, the "Political Bureau" was among the first units to
be formed.[2] After its founding, the bureau published secret bulletins
circulated internally within the IRGC, offering frank strategic assessments about the progress of the Iran-Iraq War.

The Political Bureau began evolving toward a more explicitly ideological role when the IRGC invited two philosophy professors from
Tehran University, Ahmad Fardid and Reza Davari-Ardakani, to teach
at the bureau. The main themes enumerated in the early teachings of
these two individuals were antihumanistic, antitechnological, anti-
Western, populist, insular, and at times highly nationalistic. Although
these tenets probably played a role in inspiring the initial revolutionary
fervor of the IRGC and Basij, it is questionable whether they continue
to dominate the worldview of many current and former IRGC officials,
who pride themselves on their technocratic know-how and present the
IRGC as a force for modernizing the state. If anything, these tenets
show that the IRGC's ideological outlook is not immutable, monolithic, or static; while remaining broadly faithful to the revolution's
ideals, the institution is capable of evolving in diverse and unexpected
ways.

Aside from the Political Bureau, the Office of the Representative
of the Supreme Leader in the IRGC is a major channel for indoctrination and is responsible for propagating the theory of *velayat-e faghih*
(rule of the supreme jurist). This office has emerged as a permanent
fixture in the IRGC organization and is now responsible for the Web
site and monthly magazine *Sobhe-e Sadegh*. Following the creation
of the IRGC, the office played a major role in bolstering battlefield
morale among both regular Army soldiers and Pasdaran. It deployed
over 18,000 clerics and *maddahs* (cantors) to indoctrinate fighters with

---

[1]   Article 5 from Khomeini/Revolutionary Council's original decree.

[2]   Today, Shariatmadari is the editor of the conservative newspaper *Keyhan*.

the concepts of *velayat-e faghih*, glorification of Ashura,[3] and the value of martyrdom.[4]

From this nucleus, the IRGC's ideological arm evolved into a broad network of cultural activities, institutes, think tanks, and youth camps. Many of these are conducted in tandem with the activities of other entities, such as the Islamic Republic of Iran Broadcasting (IRIB), the Ministry of Culture and Islamic Guidance, and the Islamic Propagation Organization. As noted earlier, some of these institutions, most notably the IRIB, have been led or staffed by former IRGC officers, with the effect that even training outlets not formally attached to the IRGC may be explicitly sympathetic to its institutional interests and worldview.

Among the most important ideological courses administered solely by the IRGC are those dedicated to indoctrinating young Basijis. The subject matter of these courses spans a broad gamut, from methods for organizing counter-reformist Basij student movements to vocational training and courses on speaking.[5] Underpinning many of these efforts is a focus on the family members of young Basijis as being critical pillars in the promotion of a "Basiji culture."[6]

Summer camps appear to be a key vehicle for propagating these values—and for preparing young Iranians to eventually assume the duties of armed auxiliaries to the IRGC in the regime's homeland defense strategy.[7] Commenting on these venues, the IRGC's commander for Gilan province, Colonel Sekhavatmand Davudi, noted that one of their goals is

---

[3]   The day of Ashura is the pinnacle of the rituals of mourning in the holy month of Muharram for the martyrdom of Hussein, the third Shi'ite Imam and the grandson of the prophet. It is used as a rallying point for promoting ideology of martyrdom for the just cause.

[4]   Interview with a cleric who had served as an ideological officer at war against Iraq.

[5]   Ardabil Provincial TV, "Iranian Official Praises Student Basij Activity," transcript, FBIS IAP20070831950039, August 30, 2007d.

[6]   IRNA (2007c).

[7]   Teacher's Basij Organization, "Danestanihaye morabiane tarbiati dar tarh-e misaq" (Information for "cultural" instructors in the Misaq plan), no date.

to attract the youths to the 20-million-strong army. We are responsible for doing our duty and obeying the founder of the revolution in this regard. Another one of the purposes of this plan is to give depth to religious, moral, and social orders of the youths, and we hope that with the execution of this plan we will be able to train the youths the way the revolution wants.[8]

Administered by Basij, the summer camps focus on providing young students with activities designed to inculcate them with a conservative, insular worldview, fortifying them against foreign cultural influences, such as satellite television and Internet Web sites.[9] Many are held in rural provinces, with campsites set up in several small towns. Colonel Davudi stated that, in 2007, there were 160 camps set up in Gilan province alone, with 20,000 students expected to enroll. The average age of camp participants is between 13 and 15 years.

It is important to note that the camps are not strictly ideological; they offer a social setting for sports, recreation, and the acquisition of technical skills that may be extremely appealing in remote rural provinces. According to Davudi, the summer program includes "Koranic activities, aid and relief, technical activities, book reading, sports, and camping," as well as courses in Arabic, English, chemistry, physics, and mathematics.[10] Although the camps are geared toward young Basijis, anyone who wishes to participate can enroll in the summer program.

## The IRGC Presence in Iran's Education System

Aside from running its own cultural outreach and indoctrination efforts, the IRGC and the Basij have become deeply entrenched in the Iranian education system at both the university and the high school level. Its presence in these arenas serves a twofold function. First, it fos-

---

[8]   "Rasht IRGC Commander Comments on Basij Goals in Misaq Program," *Rasht Mo'in*, FBIS IAP20070712011010, June 19, 2007.

[9]   "Persian Press: Grand Ayatollah Makarem-Shirazi Urges Exporting Basiji Ideology," *Javan*, IAP20070718011009, July 16, 2007.

[10]   "Rasht IRGC Commander Comments on Basij Goals in Misaq Program" (2007).

ters the same socialization and ideological affinity it attempts to instill through its own training activities. Secondly, it serves as a reserve countermobilization force against reform-oriented student activists.

Much of this activism in academia appears to have been facilitated by the IRGC's interference in university hiring and administration practices. In a policy reminiscent of the university purges of the early 1980s, numerous university professors and administrators have been removed from their positions and replaced with IRGC officials. Over the past few years, and especially since Ahmadinejad's election as president, academics from Tehran University, Allameh Tabataba'i University, and the Teacher Training University have been suspended or presented with early retirement letters.[11]

In the wake of these dismissals and arrests, Basij officials have begun to exert increasing influence over university life by filling the vacant professorial posts. In a statement supportive of this trend, a member of the Supreme Council for Cultural Revolution, Hojjat ol Eslam Mohammadian, explained,

> [W]e currently have 11,000 Basiji lecturers at the country's universities. . . . [A]round 20 years ago, there were only a handful of pious and religious lecturers at the country's universities. But today, the presence of a large number of such lecturers is a success for our Islamic Revolution.[12]

The Basij created the Lecturers' Basij Organization (LBO) as a means to consolidate the power of Basij academics in the field of education. The LBO reportedly has more than 15,000 members, and, according to the claims of its chief, 25 percent of Iranian lecturers are members of the LBO.[13] Besides offering career guidance to its members, the LBO provides a mechanism by which the IRGC can shape the design and implementation of university curricula—mostly to counter the

---

[11] "Iran: Daily Says Anti-Government University Teachers Increasingly Purged," *Kargozaran* [Executives], FBIS IAP20070826950116, August 25, 2007.

[12] "Iran: Daily Says Anti-Government University Teachers Increasingly Purged" (2007).

[13] "Iran: A Fourth of Iranian University Lecturers are Basij Members," *Javan*, FBIS IAP20070727011008, July 23, 2007.

flagging religiosity and ideological fervor of university students. Illustrating this, Iran's education minister recently appealed to the LBO to expand its focus on religion and Islamic culture in the academic courses of its members. Citing statistics that suggested a drop in religious convictions after graduation, he argued that the LBO's "main investment" should be on religious education while young people are still in school.[14]

While the LBO is tasked with maintaining morality and enhancing the institutional credibility of the IRGC in the upper echelons of university life, the Student Basij Organization (SBO) is the IRGC's arm for mobilizing student populations. The SBO serves as a sort of umbrella grouping for the approximately 650,000 university students throughout Iran who are Basij members, and the body is present in 700 universities.[15] The SBO enjoys a unique position on campus—what Supreme Leader Khamenei has described as a liaison between the IRGC and the university environment. During a May 2007 meeting with SBO representatives, he stated,

> The specification of this student organization is that, on the one hand, it is connected to the student environment. On the other hand, it depends on the IRGC, which is the symbol of revolutionary and brave resistance. This relationship and dependence does not mean the military nature or the restriction of this student movement; on the contrary, it joins it to a treasury of experimental, military, and disciplinary achievements gained by the IRGC that is to the benefit of the student Basij.[16]

The SBO's role as a conservative vanguard on university campuses takes two forms. First, the organization confronts reformist activists. By way of illustration, a young Basij member at Tehran University explained,

---

[14] "Persian Press: Education Minister Reveals Plans to Make Universities 'Islamic,'" *Sharq*, FBIS IAP20070803011002, July 29, 2007.

[15] Ardabil Provincial TV (2007d).

[16] "Commentary Urges Student Basij to Support Ahmadinezhad Government," *Resalat*, FBIS IAP20070531011001, May 23, 2007.

We first do it through eye contact. We let the offenders know they are doing something wrong. If they understand, it's all right. If they don't, we give a verbal warning. If that doesn't work, then we go into action. . . . We beat them so that it will have an effect on the offenders, and we beat them in a way that there will be no physical traces on the body.[17]

Second, the SBO members frequently shift their attacks from the student body to the university administration itself, particularly on social, moral, and political matters that it deems contrary to its institutional vision and that of the IRGC. For example, members of the SBO at Esfahan Medical University wrote an open letter to the university's president criticizing the lack of morality in student study-abroad programs. The letter stated,

Giving prizes for studying in a university of a non-Iranian country means permitting Iranian families to give their youths the chance to tend to corruption. This young boy or girl returns from his or her university with a lot of irregular and unacceptable morals and sits beside the pure and innocent youths of our country whose best art is studying.[18]

At times, the SBO moves beyond the university campus to level soft criticism at the regime and its bureaucracy. For example, Mohammad Mehdi Zahedi, head of the SBO at the Science and Industry University, has criticized the science ministry's crackdown on anti-regime groups while neglecting to offer increased support and funding to pro-regime organizations.[19] He also argued that student organizations should be allowed more decisionmaking power in university administration. At Imam Sadeq University, the SBO issued a statement criticiz-

---

[17] Thomas Omestad, "Iran's Culture War," *U.S. News and World Report*, July 27, 1998, pp. 33–51. The interviewee explained that beatings are conducted with "an open hand."

[18] "Persian Press: University Student Basij Urge President Act Over Studying Abroad," *Nesf-e Jahan*, FBIS IAP20070708011007, June 16, 2007.

[19] "Iran Press: Student Associations Must Share in University Policies and Decision-Making," *Kargozaran*, September 16, 2007.

ing increasing levels of economic corruption among state officials and the lack of countermeasures on the part of the administration.[20] SBO members from 162 universities released a joint statement in March 2007 insisting that Iran sever relations with the International Atomic Energy Agency.[21]

SBO members also participate in media interviews portraying a sense of revolutionary unity and support for the government. Here again, the apparent targets are student reformists; these gestures are likely intended to remind campus activists of the seeming omnipresence of Basij forces and the Basij willingness to actively confront any form of cultural or political dissent. In a 2007 opinion piece in the Tehran newspaper *Resalat*, a student Basiji argued in favor of Ahmadinejad's policies by stating, "It is the task of the Basiji student to support the government. The ninth government is a Basiji government and, just like Basij, to date it has taken brave steps to improve the conditions of the country and tangible services."[22] Similarly, student Basijis at Tehran University frequently participate in pro-government rallies and have pledged to defend Ahmadinejad's position and policies during his visits to the university.[23]

Despite the visibility and the tenor of Basij student activism, the university campuses by no means have fallen completely under their sway. Indeed, a broad spectrum of student groups continue to vie with the SBO, illustrating that certain sectors in Iranian intellectual and societal life remain contested arenas, despite the extensive reach of the IRGC's indoctrination efforts. A September 2007 article in the Iranian daily *E'temad-e Melli,* which was founded by the prominent reformist and former Parliamentary Speaker Mehdi Karrubi, describes the

---

[20]   Open Source Center, "Highlights: Iran Economic Sanctions, Government Corruption 25–31 Oct 07," FBIS IAP20071116306003, *OSC Summary in Persian*, October 25–31, 2007c.

[21]   "Mobilization Force Demands Halt of Cooperation with IAEA," Fars News Agency (Internet Version), FBIS IAP20070327950047, March 27, 2007.

[22]   "Commentary Urges Student Basij to Support Ahmadinezhad Government" (2007).

[23]   "Student Unrest Marks Iran President's University Lecture," BBC World Monitoring, FEA20071008352786-OSC Feature, October 8, 2007.

three other major university student unions present on the country's campuses:[24]

- *The Islamic Association of Students.* This group represents the traditional conservatives in Iranian politics (as distinguished from the radical ideology that appears to be more present among members of the SBO).
- *The Office for Consolidating Unity.* This organization has a traditional leftist ideology and is said to work for a "freedom-centered concept" in the universities.
- *The Office for Consolidating Democracy (OCD).* The OCD has a "new left" ideology and seeks to promote civil society in Iran.

The third of these, the OCD, is currently the main competitor to the SBO on Iranian campuses. The Islamic Association of Students and the Office for Consolidating Unity are both plagued by internal divisions and dissension that weaken their ability to expand their support base. The OCD's strength is probably of greatest concern to the IRGC and SBO because its ideology is completely antithetical to the ideals of the revolution as interpreted by the Basij. A number of pro-regime commentators in the Iranian press have indeed warned their readers that a dangerous "new left" ideology in Iranian universities poses a serious threat to revolutionary ideals.

Recently, senior Basij officials have called for the expansion of SBO offices outside of the university setting. A representative from Hormozgan province stated in February 2007, "The student branch of the Basij Force must be founded in all high schools, especially in boarding schools. We must reach the point that the branches of Basij Force are opened in high schools as immediately as the high schools are opened."[25] Commander of the Basij in Hormozgan, General Dehqan, emphasized the importance of the Basij in high schools by stating,

---

[24] "Paper Analyses Activities of Political Student Organizations in Iran," *E'temad-e Melli* (Tehran), FBIS IAP20070905950036, September 4, 2007.

[25] "Persian Press: Official Says High Schools Should Have Basij Force Branches," *Marjan*, FBIS IAP20070319005010, February 24, 2007.

"Basijis do miracles in every field they are involved. Without the Basij Force our Islamic system has not been able to survive."[26]

## The "Ten-Million-Man Army": The IRGC's Role in Popular Paramilitary Training

As noted previously, one of the goals of this youth-oriented outreach is to foster social networks, esprit de corps, and a reverence for the state that eventually compels them to enroll in military training—either in the Basij itself or through the professional IRGC. The youth socialization process also holds the promise of upward mobility, offering the prospect of an officer commission, the acquisition of technical skills, and increased marketability.[27] This function appears particularly important in co-opting groups from the rural periphery into the "center"— unlike the militaries of certain Arab states, the IRGC's demographic composition is geographically diverse, incorporating nearly all of Iran's provinces.

Today, the IRGC and Basij conduct regular paramilitary training throughout Iran for both active and potential members, drawn from a broad spectrum of Iranian society—ranging from the rural classes and provincial tribes to students and factory workers. About 600,000 of the 3 million active members of the Basij are part of armed paramilitary units that regularly take part in this military training, which includes military exercises and drills.[28] This paramilitary wing is made up of a mix of male *ashura* battalions and female *zahra* battalions, as well as *karbala* and *zolfaqar* special combat groups.[29] Accounts in the

---

[26] "Persian Press: Official Says High Schools Should Have Basij Force Branches" (2007).

[27] Comments of an Iranian-born scholar at a RAND-sponsored conference, Rome, Italy, October 29, 2007.

[28] Vision of the Islamic Republic of Iran Sistan-Baluchestan Provincial TV (2007a); "Iran: Commander Says Militia Has More Than 12 Million Forces," Open Source Center, FBIS IAP20070523950091, May 23, 2007a.

[29] Open Source Center, "Iran: Iranian TV Features Basij Parades Across Iran," *OSC Report in Persian*, IAP20071210598001, November 26, 2007h.

contemporary Iranian press suggest that the IRGC has four purposes in mind when it carries out its military training exercises and drills for Basij volunteers throughout Iran: equipping Basij members to participate in the regime's homeland defense strategy; training them for disaster-relief operations; preparing them to defend the regime against a so-called "soft coup," i.e., U.S. efforts to erode revolutionary values through the promotion of civil society and the fostering of ethnic dissent; and providing an additional venue for inculcating the populace with the IRGC's institutional values.

### Increasing the Basij's Capability to Conduct Asymmetric Homeland Defense

Based on available open-source reporting, Iran's national defense strategy rests on its ability to inflict an exorbitant cost on an invader as a deterrent and, if an invasion comes, to draw out the campaign to the extent that the invader loses the mettle to pursue its objectives to their conclusion. The Basij are critical pillars of this strategy, responsible for implementing Iranian such doctrinal concepts as "mosaic defense" and "spontaneous battle."[30] According to these concepts, partisan and irregular units, recruited from the population by the Basij, would fall back behind an advancing army, harassing its rear area, attacking its lines of communication, and essentially rendering an occupation untenable through extended attrition.

Much of this strategy hinges on indoctrinating Basij and partisan units with superior morale or "strategic patience," which the IRGC leadership sees as the ultimate center of gravity on the battlefield.[31] The lessons of the 2006 Lebanon war appear to have shaped this thinking: The IRGC often paints the Basij as roughly analogous to the Lebanese Hizballah in their ability to mobilize popular sympathy and wage a sophisticated guerrilla campaign against a better-equipped adversary.[32]

---

[30]  Vision of the Islamic Republic of Iran Network (2005).

[31]  "Iran: A Fourth of Iranian University Lecturers are Basij Members" (2007).

[32]  Iran's possible strategy of "passive defense," which aims to maintain military communications and government authority over Iran's territory, may have been tested and/or inspired by Hezbollah's guerrilla war against Israel in 2006. Hezbollah units, drawn from local vil-

According to the commander of the Basij Resistance Force of the IRGC in Sistan-Baluchestan Province, "the victory of Lebanon's Hezbollah in the 33-day war against Israeli troops was a result of passive defense," a strategy which the Basij appears to be pursuing in individual Iranian provinces.

This comparison appears to be misplaced, exaggerating the Basij's cohesion and competence as a paramilitary force, as well as its ability to sustain long-term support from a populace whose views toward the organization seem unevenly split between urban and rural sectors. Several other events and developments raise further questions about the ideological fortitude and combat capacity within the Basij ranks:

- In 2004, the regime instituted a constitutional amendment to the draft law, allowing young men wishing to avoid active military service to fulfill their obligations in the Basij. The net effect of this development may be to erode the unit cohesion of Basij units and their collective morale as their ranks become swelled with those seeking a "way out" from conscription in the regular forces.
- Anecdotal reporting suggests that some Basijis attend periodic military training and indoctrination simply to obtain economic benefits, such as scholarships and loans. Whether or not these perks are sufficient to sustain the morale of the force throughout an extended campaign is an open question.
- Basij units are lightly armed, and most Basij personnel do not get significant military training.

Despite these shortcomings, the Basij still provide a large pool of manpower that is at least nominally familiar with the use of light infantry weapons that can form the nucleus of regional resistance movements. If only a fraction of the individuals on the Basij payroll remain

---

lages, fought Israeli forces without much apparent central oversight. In the case of an invasion, Iran's Basij forces and the IRGC may fight in a similar fashion in order to withstand possible U.S. attempts to destroy Iran's command and control capabilities. See Vision of the Islamic Republic of Iran Sistan-Baluchestan Provincial TV, "Iran: 'Passive Defense' Contract Held in Southeast," Open Source Center, IAP20080102950084, January 1, 2008.

loyal to the Iranian clerical regime and take up arms, there would be a significant post-conflict resistance movement in Iran.[33]

## Disaster-Relief Training

Aside from this military function, the Basij are trained in disaster-relief operations. Press coverage of several 2007 Basij training exercises describes disaster-relief and humanitarian assistance as principal foci of these drills. Maintaining social order in disaster zones and distributing relief and medical supplies are among the tasks that the Basij volunteers practiced. There is an important regime-stability component to this training: Natural disasters are often opportunities for marginalized Iranian rural groups to express their frustrations with the failings of the central government in other areas. It is imperative, therefore, that as the first responders of the regime, the Basij are seen as well trained, proficient, rapid, and sympathetic to local sensitivities. Perhaps more than any other function, the emergency-relief role is an opportunity for the IRGC, via the Basij, to present a benign and sympathetic face to the Iranian populace.

## Protection Against Soft Coups

A third function of Basij popular training is to deter and defeat "soft-coup" attempts within Iran—meaning the formation of dissident intellectual groupings, civil society, and reform-oriented student organizations. As noted earlier, there is an explicit fear among conservative regime figures that reformist press outlets, Western-supported nongovernmental organizations, and liberal intellectuals are conspiring to erode and dismantle the foundations of the Islamic Republic in a manner akin to the "color revolutions" that swept parts of the former Soviet Union in 2003–2005. Basij battalions are seen as a counter-mobilizing force against this effort, both through their expansive cultural education and indoctrination and also in the form of a visible street presence.

---

[33] "Persian Press: Education Minister Reveals Plans to Make Universities 'Islamic'" (2007).

**Additional Cultural Education**

Along these lines, the IRGC intends for Basij popular military training to serve as the principle medium for instilling ideological conformity and loyalty to the regime in Iran's rapidly growing youth population. In addition to instruction in weapon handling and small-unit tactics, Basij military training exercises include ideological and religious lectures. As noted earlier, these lectures, in the minds of the Basij leaders, offer a means of counteracting harmful foreign cultural influences that are viewed as a threat to the ideals of the revolution. Foreign Web sites and DVDs are seen as special threats to Iranian youth. It is important to note the opportunity costs associated with this focus on ideological conformity; in the Basij's monthly training cycle, time devoted to religious classes and ideological lectures means time not spent developing individual small-arms proficiency, exercising in unit formations, and other basic combat skills.

A survey of recent reporting on Basij exercises in the open press sheds light on the diverse roles of this paramilitary force, as well as the inherent tension between indoctrination and combat readiness that characterizes its training. In 2007, the Basij conducted a number of large-scale popular training exercises:

- In late July, the Basij units of the West Azerbaijan province participated in a four-day training course that included instruction on asymmetric warfare, direction finding, night combat tactics, and politics and ideology.[34]
- In early August, the Basij of Tehran's Meqdad region conducted a large 40-battalion exercise called "Appointment of the Prophet Mohammad Desert Maneuver" that included work in "combat, ambush, logistics, operations, and reconnaissance."[35]

---

[34]  Vision of the Islamic Republic of Iran West Azarbayjan Provincial TV, "Paramilitaries in Iranian West Azarbayjan Province Attend Training Courses," Open Source Center, FBIS IAP 20070726950056, July 25, 2007.

[35]  IRNA, "Iran: Forty Battalions of Basij Force Carry Out Exercise in Tehran Region," Open Source Center, FBIS IAP20070809950102, August 9, 2007b.

- Also early in August, the Basij forces of East Azerbaijan province undertook four days of drills that focused on civil defense training and rescue operations during natural disasters.[36]
- In mid-August, the Basij Resistance Forces of Ardabil province conducted a four-day military exercise code-named "Unity," during which *ashura* and *zahra* personnel from the area practiced "troop call up, organization of the forces, operations, and preparation for deterrence operations."[37]

## The IRGC Media Apparatus: Formal and Informal Influences

In tandem with its education and paramilitary training, the IRGC has built a vast media apparatus that allows it to propagate its vision of the Islamic Republic of Iran and highlight its institutional legitimacy to multiple sectors of the population.

Chief among its various outlets is its Web site and weekly magazine, *Sobh-e Sadegh,* sponsored by the Supreme Leader's representative to the IRGC. The weekly is a conservative source that reports on current news and political issues, but its principle focus is on highlighting the IRGC's positive contributions to bettering the nation and the lives of its citizens.

The magazine has 16 sections: "First News," "Second News," "IRGC," "Basij," "Second Look at the Media," "Moral Issues," "Analytical Reports," "News Reports," "International Issues," "Weekly Debate," "Political Workshop," "History," "Art," "Viewers," "Social Issues," and a "Special Issues" section composed of a series of short reports dealing with military, cultural, and religious subjects, including the IRGC's engineering achievements and news coverage of Basij activities throughout the country. A November 2007 edition of the

---

[36] IRNA, "Iranian Paramilitaries Start Drills in East Azarbayjan," Open Source Center, FBIS IAP20070809950061, August 8, 2007a.

[37] Ardabil Provincial TV, "Iran: Volunteer Force to Hold Military Drills in Northwestern Border Province," Open Source Center, FBIS IAP20070812950082, August 10, 2007c.

magazine covered a variety of topics, including a memorial for war martyrs, budget management of IRGC-related foundations, the role of the Basij in the media, and a general discussion of international political issues.[38] *Sobh-e Sadegh* also has a link to the Web site Ofogh (Horizon), which maintains ties to IRGC-affiliated construction companies, such as Khatam al-Anbia (discussed at length later).[39]

Former and current IRGC officials also operate a number of popular news outlets and specialized Web sites:

- In 2002, former IRGC commander and current Secretary of the Expediency Council Mohsen Rezai launched the conservative Baztab Web site (currently known as Tabnak) in response to a proliferation of reformist sites.[40]
- The influential *Keyhan* newspaper is directed by former IRGC member Hossein Shariatmadari. *Keyhan* distributes several weekly publications, as well as Arabic and English editions, while Shariatmadari himself enjoys media exposure through the Sharif News Web site run by the Sharif Industrial University SBO. The site frequently highlights his articles in conjunction with news reports.[41] Although Shariatmadari and Rezai are rivals, they are nevertheless part of the broad (and non-monolothic) IRGC network.
- Former IRGC commander Ezatollah Zarghami directs IRIB, the state's official broadcasting service. Like his predecessor Ali Larijani, also a former IRGC officer, Zarghami has claimed that confronting the foreign cultural onslaught is a key component of IRIB's mission. The IRIB currently controls five nationwide

---

[38] *Sobh-e Sadegh*, weekly magazine, November 17, 2007.

[39] "Iran: Profile of IRGC-Linked Website, Sobhe-Sadegh," OSC Media Aid in English, GMF20060427388002, April 27, 2006.

[40] "Website Forecasts Central Bank Chief as Next Victim of Iran's Cabinet Reshuffle," Tehran Baztab, FBIS IAP20070818950092, August 17, 2007.

[41] "BBC Monitoring: Iran Media Guide," Caversham BBC Monitoring in English, FBIS IAP20070327950024, March 27, 2007. See also "Iran: Profile of IRGC-Linked Website, Sobhe-Sadegh" (2006).

television channels, including a 24-hour news service and several provincial stations.[42]

- In addition, the IRGC maintains a Web site called Farhang-e Isaar (Culture of Self-Sacrifice), which is aimed at the promotion of the culture of martyrdom and self-sacrifice. The Web site is controlled by the Council of Coordination and Supervision of the Promotion of the Culture of Martyrdom and Self-Sacrifice.[43]
- The Basij News Agency also maintains a Web site to publicize news about ongoing activities. In September 2007, a Basij public relations official said that a weekly publication is also being developed.[44]

In areas where they lack direct media control, IRGC and Basij officials heavily publicize the need for media cooperation in reporting on public-service activities, as well as in propagating the "culture of sacred defense" throughout Iranian society, particularly in Iran's rural areas. Highlighting this point, former IRGC commander-in-chief Rahim Safavi has urged various non-IRGC news outlets to focus on disseminating the message of the IRGC and the Islamic Revolution. For example, in an interview with Esfahan provincial television station Voice and Vision, he said,

> I hope that all our media sources will understand properly the new conditions that we are facing both inside and outside our borders, carry out their information-dissemination duties well, warm the hearts of our nation, and create happiness and enthusiasm in the general public, particularly the youth.[45]

Colonel Karim Qanbarnezhad of the Ardabil Basij recently called on the media to focus on the propagation of Islamic culture and dis-

---

[42] "BBC Monitoring: Iran Media Guide" (2007).

[43] Farhang-e Isaar, homepage.

[44] "Iranian Official Heralds New Basij News Agency, Weekly," *Keyhan* (Tehran), FBIS IAP20070903950076, September 3, 2007.

[45] Vision of the Islamic Republic of Iran Sistan-Baluchestan Provincial TV (2007a).

seminate information on the Iran-Iraq War and the role of the IRGC and Basij in defending the country. He asked Iranian journalists to document the IRGC's current work and insisted that the IRGC is willing to accept media criticism and recommendations regarding its role as a guardian of Islamic culture.[46]

Basij commander Mehdi Sa'adati of Khuzestan province echoed similar sentiments during a provincial conference of Basij officials and local media outlets. Sa'adati alleged that Iran's enemies are engaged in a "media war" to weaken the Islamic Republic and emphasized the importance of the Iranian press in protecting the country's religious and cultural values. He stressed the need for "bilateral relations" between the media and the Basij to promote Basij culture and public service.[47] Similarly, IRGC General Bahman Reyhani of the Kermanshah region recently called on media outlets to play a more effective role in countering the "cultural war" provoked by Western influences.[48]

Even IRGC commander Jafari has been active in requesting enhanced collaboration between media sources and local Basij representatives. During an October 2007 conference on media and the Basij held in Khorasan province, he advanced the Islamic principle of "enjoining virtue, proscribing vice" and said,

> The mass media must enjoy the spirit and culture of the Basij, and on that basis, they should embark on fulfilling their important role to promote and spread these Islamic Revolutionary ideals and aspirations across the society.[49]

---

[46]   IRNA, "Iranian Provincial Commander Calls for More Cooperation with Media," FBIS IAP20070926950125, September 25, 2007d.

[47]   Ahvaz Vision of the Islamic Republic of Iran Khuzestan Provincial TV, "Iranian Khuzestan Basij Commander Meets Media, Press," FBIS IAP20071122950059, November 21, 2007.

[48]   Open Source Center, "Selection List—Persian Press Menu 17 Nov 07," OSC Summary in Persian, IAP20071117011005, November 17, 2007f.

[49]   "Iran: Guards Commander Praises Government's Focus on Islamic Values," Iran (Tehran), FBIS IAP20071102950012, October 27, 2007.

To improve collaboration between journalists and rural IRGC and Basij representatives, the IRGC and Basij sponsor a number of media workshops. To consolidate participation in these workshops, the Basij established the Correspondents' Club for writers and reporters affiliated with the IRGC and/or Basij. In November 2007, more than 150 journalists attended one such workshop in Ardabil province that offered training and guidance on reporting techniques. During the proceedings, an official from the Office of the Representative of the Supreme Leader to the Ardabil IRGC called for increased cooperation between the local media and the Basij Correspondents' Club to publish "round-the-clock" updates on the activities of the Basij and IRGC in Ardabil province.[50] Other IRGC speakers utilized the workshop as an opportunity to express the belief that safeguarding Islamic values requires media attentiveness to the prominent role of the IRGC and Basij in society.

A similar workshop was sponsored by the IRGC's Political Bureau at around the same time. Approximately 25 reporters attended the weeklong training, which covered techniques for collecting and disseminating news stories, as well as interviewing techniques.[51]

## Censorship of Independent Media Outlets

Where it cannot actively solicit media cooperation and favorable coverage, the IRGC and Basij are well equipped for and frequently predisposed toward censorship. This is particularly the case concerning Internet usage. For example, the IRGC plays a role in monitoring Internet communications to mitigate the influx of corrupting foreign ideals and antiregime material.[52] In this effort, it coordinates closely with other security entities. In a 2007 interview, the head of the Internet section

---

[50]  IRNA, "Workshop in Ardabil on Reporting About Paramilitary Forces' Activities," FBIS IAP20071114950125, November 14, 2007e.

[51]  Open Source Center, "Highlights: Iranian Media Developments, November 2007," OSC Summary in Persian, IAP20071205584001, December 5, 2007i.

[52]  "BBC Monitoring: Iran Media Guide" (2007).

of the Tehran Public and Revolutionary Prosecutor's office explained, "On the whole, filtering is being carried out between . . . the government, the judiciary, the officials of the law-enforcement forces and the Basij."[53] A five-person committee whose members are appointed by the Islamic Propaganda Organization and a representative of the Supreme Cultural Revolution Council act as the final authority in deciding which Web sites contain illicit material. Filtered content is mostly comprised of "key scientific terms" used on Web sites unaffiliated with the scientific research community and material indicative of illicit telecommunication services.

Taken in sum, the IRGC's training, indoctrination, and media outreach form an important pillar of its outreach to the Iranian populace. It is ultimately difficult, however, to assess the degree to which population segments embrace its ideology or whether its communication efforts have affected positive shifts in public opinion about IRGC. On this issue, popular sentiment may be more favorably predisposed toward the Pasdaran on the basis of its economic activities and the co-option of various business sectors into its constellation of affiliated companies, which present more tangible benefits than ideology. At the same time, this economic expansion presents a double-edged sword with the capacity to antagonize traditional business and merchant elites, thereby mitigating whatever favorable views were accumulated during its indoctrination activities. It is to this dynamic that we now turn.

---

[53] "Official Provides Details About Internet Filtering," *E'ternad* (Internet Version), FBIS IAP20070414950102, April 14, 2007.

# CHAPTER FIVE

# Economic Expansion: The IRGC's Business Conglomerate and Public Works

From laser eye surgery and construction to automobile manufacturing and real estate, the IRGC has extended its influence into virtually every sector of the Iranian market. Perhaps more than any other area of its domestic involvement, its business activities represent the multidimensional nature of the institution. The commercialization of the IRGC has the potential to broaden the circle of its popular support by co-opting existing financial elites into its constellation of subsidiary companies and subcontractors. Similarly, through the socialization and recruitment of rural and lower-class populations into the Basij—frequently accompanied by technical job training, scholarships, and other financial benefits—the IRGC offers the promise of societal mobility to those who would otherwise be denied it. Added to this image of egalitarianism is the IRGC's role in building up the rural economy through the numerous public-works projects carried out by the Basij.

The subtext of this apparent economic populism is, of course, the IRGC's control of Iran's shadow economy—the illicit smuggling networks, kickbacks, no-bid contracts, and the accumulation of wealth by its senior officials that remains largely unseen by the Iranian population. Added to this is the inevitable displacement of traditional business elites by its monopolization of key financial sectors. Yet reports of opposition to this growing dominance remain largely at the anecdotal level. To determine how and in what form the IRGC's economic expansion can both cultivate legitimacy and provoke dissent, it is necessary to canvass the full sweep of its business interests and public works.

## Origins of the IRGC's Economic Activities

The roots of the IRGC's entry into the economic realm lie in the wake of the Iran-Iraq War, when Supreme Leader Khamenei instituted a formal ranking system into what had been a flat IRGC organization. The introduction of a genuine hierarchy began the process of inculcating the notion of perquisites, privileges, and status for the senior leadership of the IRGC into its institutional culture. The profit motive became even more pronounced in the 1992–1993 period, when business-savvy President Rafsanjani initiated the idea of involving government organizations in business transactions as a way to generate independent income.[1] By the late 1990s, the process of economic expansion had begun in earnest, and it has accelerated even more during the Ahmadinejad presidency, which has favored the IRGC by offering it numerous lucrative no-bid contracts, especially in the areas of oil and natural gas extraction, pipeline construction, and large-scale infrastructure development.[2]

It is important to note that the IRGC's expansion into the business sector harnessed the informal social networks that had developed among veterans and former officials. Thus, when we describe the IRGC's economic influence, we use a very broad definition that captures the informality of its reach. Moreover, the model of a shadow economy and the creation of networks of patronage and clientage are roughly analogous to an institution that has long been a feature of Iran's postrevolutionary landscape—the *bonyads,* or parastatal, revolu-

---

[1]  Sazegara (2006).

[2]  Gharargah-e Sazandegiye Khatam al-Anbia (Ghorb) (2007); National Iranian Gas Company, "Ba hozur-e vazir-e naft va farmandeye kolle sepah-e pasdaran: emza-e moghavelenameye projeye ehdas-e khat lule-e haftom-e sarasari-e gas" (The seventh national gas pipeline contract was signed in presence of the minister of oil and the head of IRGC), June 7, 2007; Technology Development of Iranian Oil Industry, *Negahi be amalkard-e sherkat-e melli naft dar sal-e 1385* (National Iranian Oil Company outlook 2006), 2006; Iran Economic News Agency, "Tarh-e LNG 2 va 3 emza shod" (LNG 2 and 3 plans were signed), no date; Ministry of Oil News Agency, "Emza-e Gharardad-e Shirinsaziy-e Gas projey-e Iran LNG" (The contract of gas sweetening of Iran's LNG project was signed), November 4, 2007; BBC News Persian, "Gharardad-e jadid-e tosee-ye meidan-e gazi-e pars-e jonoubi" (Pars Jonoubi new gas contract), May 1, 2005.

tionary foundations that constitute vast reservoirs of wealth controlled by key clerics, ostensibly for charitable purposes. Indeed, one scholar remarked that the IRGC's affiliated companies were effectively "militarized bonyads."[3]

## Foundations (Bonyads)

The bonyads under the Islamic Republic are not necessarily a new phenonmenon, but rather are a continuation of informal and extralegal economic networks from the shah's reign. The Pahlavi Foundation under the shah, for example, was direct predecessor of such Islamic bonyads as the Mostazafan Foundation.[4] After the shah's overthrow, the Pahlavi Foundation's assets were taken over by the newly created Mostazafan Foundation.

Two important bonyads, which are not directly controlled by the IRGC but are indirectly influenced by it, are the Bonyad Mostazafan (Foundation of the Oppressed or The Mostazafan Foundation) and the Bonyad Shahid va Omur-e Janbazan (Foundation of Martyrs and Veterans Affairs). The Bonyad Mostazafan is the largest foundation in Iran and is also well integrated into the Iranian economy. It officially operates as a nongovernmental organization, though it is directly supervised by the Supreme Leader, who appoints its director.[5] The current director of Mostazafan is Mohammad Forouzandeh, the former head of the Ministry of Defense and Armed Forces Logistics and a former IRGC officer.[6]

According to one of the foundation's former directors, Mohsen Rafiqdust, Mostazafan allocates 50 percent of its profits to providing

---

[3]    Comments by an Iranian-born scholar at a RAND-sponsored conference, Rome, Italy, October 29, 2007.

[4]    "Nobody Influences Me!" *Time Magazine*, December 10, 1979.

[5]    "Bonyads Ripe for Restructuring," Middle East Data Project, Inc., Iran Brief 8, December 1999.

[6]    Mehdi Khalaji, "Iran's Revolutionary Guard Corps, Inc.," Washington Institute for Near East Policy, *PolicyWatch*, No. 1273, August 17, 2007.

aid to the needy in the form of low-interest loans or monthly pensions, while it invests the remaining 50 percent in its various subsidiaries.[7] It owns and operates approximately 350 subsidiary and affiliate companies in numerous industries including agriculture, industry, transportation, and tourism.[8] Mostazafan's largest subsidiary is the Agricultural and Food Industries Organization (AFIO), which owns more than 115 additional companies. Some of the foundation's contract work also includes large engineering projects, such as the construction of Terminal One of the Imam Khomeini International Airport.[9]

Mostazafan also has a history of soliciting contract work abroad. It currently maintains economic connections with countries in the Middle East, Europe, Africa, and South Asia, as well as in Russia and other former states of the Soviet Union. Mostazafan subsidiaries pursued contracts in the late 1990s to construct a railway system and urban rail system and to manage a livestock project in Libya.[10] More recently, the General Mechanic Civil and Housing Organization, another Mostazafan subsidiary, began work in 2004 on a $30 million, 36-month contract to build a 37-km road into the Hajar mountains in the United Arab Emirates. The road was one of multiple phases in the construction of the Jebel Jais mountain resort.[11]

Some reports allege that Mostazafan facilitated the development of psuedosecret organizations, such as the Nur Foundation, which was reportedly established in 1999 to import sugar, construction materials, and pharmaceuticals. It is also said to maintain an office near a suspected nuclear research laboratory in Tehran.[12]

---

[7]   Robert Fisk, "War Wounded Find Comfort from Billion-Dollar Man," *The Independent*, May 26, 1995.

[8]   Mostazafan Foundation, homepage, 2008.

[9]   "Turkish Firm Signs up for Tehran Airport," *Middle East Economic Digest*, April 30, 2004.

[10]   "Iran Clinches Cement Contract," *Middle East Economic Digest*, January 10, 1997.

[11]   "RAK Unveils Multi-Billion Dollar Plans," *Middle East Economic Digest*, June 3, 2005.

[12]   Open Source Center, "Iran: Mostazafan va Janbazan Supports Veterans, Covert Activities," May 2, 2006.

In addition to Bonyad Mostazafan, the Bonyad Shahid maintains a strong link to the IRGC, with former IRGC Air Force commander Hossein Dehghan acting as its president. Shahid gives home loans to thousands of Basijis and the families of martyrs. It has reportedly loaned 120 million rials to urban families and 150 million rials to rural families.[13] Shahid is also involved in numerous economic endeavors, including participation in a joint venture with the Industrial Development and Renovation Organization and Defense Ministry subsidiary, the Iran Electronic Development Company. In March 2004, this company was part of a consortium that won a mobile-phone license from the Iranian government, but the deal fell through because of political objections.[14]

## Construction, Engineering, and Manufacturing Companies

The IRGC's industrial activities began not long after the Iran-Iraq War, when President Rafsanjani's government encouraged the IRGC to use economic activities to bolster its budget.[15] The corps took control of several confiscated factories and established the *moavenat khodkafaee* (headquarters of self-sufficiency) and *moavenat bassazi* (headquarters of reconstruction). These two headquarters established various companies active in the agriculture, industrial, mining, transportation, road construction, import, and export sectors.[16] Shortly thereafter, the IRGC established a reconstruction headquarters, which operated within the IRGC's air force, navy, ground force, and Basij. In 1990, the headquarters became *gharargah sazandegi khatam alanbia*, abbreviated as Ghorb. Ghorb, also known as Khatam al-Anbia, established several companies

---

13  "Iran: Profile of IRGC-Linked Website, Sobhe-Sadegh" (2006).

14  "Special Report: Iran," *Middle East Economic Digest*, August 24–30, 2007.

15  Sazegara (2006).

16  Behrouz Khaligh, "Changes in the Political Structure of the Islamic Republic: From the Clerical Oligarchy to the Oligarchy of the Clerics and Guards," Akhbar e Rouz, July 4, 2006a.

active in agriculture, industry, mining, road building, transportation, import, export, education, and culture.[17]

Khatam al-Anbia has since become one of Iran's largest contractors in industrial and development projects, and today is considered the IRGC's major engineering arm,[18] not unlike the U.S. Army Corps of Engineers. IRGC commander Sattar Vafaei stated in an interview that about 25,000 engineers and staff work for Khatam al-Anbia. Ten percent of these personnel are IRGC members and the rest are contractors. The company has launched an official Web site, as well as an internal journal called *Road and Tunnel Magazine*, though neither has published numbers reflecting the company's assets.

According to the Khatam al-Anbia Web site, the company

- has been awarded more than 750 contracts in different construction fields, including dams; water diversion systems; highways; tunnels; buildings; heavy-duty structures; three-dimensional trusses; offshore construction; water supply systems; and water, gas, and oil main pipelines
- has completed 150 projects involving technical consulting and supervision
- is currently implementing 21 new projects, many of which are slated for rural areas.[19]

The Ministry of Oil, Transportation, and Energy and the mayor of Tehran have signed several contracts with the IRGC through Khatam al-Anbia. These projects are contracted to Khatam al-Anbia and are performed either by its subsidiaries or by private companies contracted by Khatam al-Anbia. The Khatam Web site lists some of these companies, as well as the nature of their work. Two of the most prominent Khatam subsidiaries are Sepasad and Hara; the former is currently construct-

---

[17]  Gharargah-e Sazandegiye Khatam al-Anbia (Ghorb) homepage.

[18]  Pars Special Economic Energy Zone, "Didar-e Jami az maghamat-e arshad-e sepah pasdaran as tasisat-e parse jonubi" (Visit of IRGC top rank officials from Pars Jonoubi establishments), May 29, 2007.

[19]  Gharargah-e Sazandegiye Khatam al-Anbia (Ghorb), homepage.

ing Line Seven of the Tehran Metro,[20] while the latter directs tunnel construction and excavation operations throughout the country. Other projects performed by Khatam subsidiaries include the construction of part of the Tehran-Tabriz railway,[21] the Karkheh dam,[22] reserve packages and a jetty in the Pars Jonoubi Gas field,[23] and a 900-km gas pipeline from Asaluye to Iranshahr.[24] Subsidiaries are also engaged in several hydroelectric and dam-construction projects in West Azarbaijan, Kordestan, Kermanshah, Ilam, Lorestan, and Khuzestan.[25]

Khatam al-Anbia is highly active in the oil sector and is said to be operating as the sole contractor for Iran's gas industry.[26] The agency's deputy director for reconstruction, IRGC Brigadier Abdolreza Abedzadeh, said that the company had 247 ongoing "industrial and mining" projects and had completed 1,220 projects since 1990.[27] Iran's oil ministry has signed a number of no-bid contracts with the company worth billions of dollars. Government officials claim that these contracts were awarded because of the lower cost offered by the IRGC, its skilled corps of engineers, its experience with large projects, and its

---

[20] International Crisis Group (2007). See also "Haftomin khate metroye Iran ra sepah misazad" (7th line of Tehran Metro to be built by IRGC), *Keyhan*, April 20, 2006.

[21] Tehran City Hall Information Management Organization, "Bakhsi az khat-e ahane Tehran Tabriz be zire zamin montaghel mishavad," February 13, 2007.

[22] "Dam Project Goes to Revolutionary Guards," *Middle East Economic Digest*, October 7, 1994.

[23] "Gharardad-e Shirinsaziye gase faze 12 parse jonubi emza shod" (The Agreement on the Sweetening of Gas from South Pars Phase 12 Has Been Signed), *Shana*, November 4, 2007.

[24] BBC News Persian, "Gharardad-e 1.3 milliard dollari sepah ba vezarat-e naft" (The $1.3 Billion Agreement Between the Guards and the Oil Ministry), May 8, 2006. See also Shahrgone, "Vagozari-e ehdas-e khat-e lule-e gaz be sepah bedune anjame tashrifat-e monaghese," no date.

[25] Gharargah-e Sazandegiye Khatam al-Anbia (Ghorb), homepage.

[26] Open Source Center (2007c).

[27] Khalaji (2007). See also Matthew Levitt, "Make Iran Feel the Pain," *Wall Street Journal Europe*, July 2, 2007; Alireza Jafarzadeh, "Islamic Revolutionary Guards Corp (IRGC): Control Over All Aspects of the Iranian Regime," Strategic Policy Consulting, statement National Press Club meeting, August 22, 2007; and Kim Murphy, "Iran's Guard Builds a Fiscal Empire," *Los Angeles Times*, August 26, 2007.

access to heavy machinery and sizable assets.[28] In one such contract, the ministry awarded Khatam $1.3 billion to build the aforementioned 900-km natural gas pipeline to transfer 5 million cubic meters of gas from Asaluyeh in the province of Bushehr to Iranshahr in the province of Sistan and Baluchestan. When pressed as to why the ministry waived the bidding requirement for Khatam al-Anbia, a ministry representative claimed that providing gas to underprivileged regions was an urgent necessity and that a formal bidding process would have taken more than a year to complete.[29] An additional $2.5 billion contract was awarded to Khatam al-Anbia without a bid to finish phases 15 and 16 of the Pars Jonoubi (South Pars) oil field.[30]

Khatam al-Anbia deputy director Abdolreza Abedzadeh recently told the Iranian press that 70 percent of Khatam's business is military related. However, employees are often less forthcoming. When questioned as to the nature of the work, company employee and civil engineer Mohammadreza Rajabalinejad informed the *Wall Street Journal*, "I'm not allowed to tell you anything."[31] Other employees are typically unwilling to discuss the nature of Khatam's contracts as well.[32] Members of the Iranian press have complained that reporters "have repeatedly asked this company to provide more detailed information on the company and the exact figures for completed projects, the number of personnel, and the problems facing this major contractor, but the company has refused to comply."[33]

---

[28] "Namayandeye vali faghi dar sepah-e padaran: sepah nabayad abzar-e tashakkolhaye siasi shaved" (Representative of the Supreme Leader to the IRGC: The IRGC should not get involved in politics), *Sharq*, July 2006.

[29] National Iranian Gas Company (2006).

[30] Ministry of Oil News Agency (2007). See also Pars Special Economic Energy Zone (2007) and BBC News Persian (2005).

[31] Andrew Higgins, "As Hard-Liners Rise, Shadowy Revolutionary Guard Muscles in on Airport and Nabs Energy Deals; Dawn Clash Over a Drilling Rig in the Persian Gulf," *Wall Street Journal*, October 14, 2006.

[32] Higgins (2006).

[33] Open Source Center (2007c).

In an interview with the newspaper *Sharq*, Abedzadeh answered questions regarding the company's funding and employment and also responded to allegations that the company had accepted certain government contracts without engaging in a formal bidding process. He also admitted to receiving a no-bid contract for the Asaluyeh-Iranshahr pipeline project and justified the process by claiming that "[the government has] seen our work. We must have done something for them to be willing to award us the contract without bidding."[34] He also acknowledged winning the no-bid contract for phases 15 and 16 of the South Pars oil field, explaining that Pars Oil and Gas had "promised the project" to Khatam even before a foreign partner had pulled out of the contract for which Khatam had bid and subsequently won. Abedzadeh went on to explain,

> So the foreign company withdrew from the consortium. What were we supposed to do? . . . We spoke with Pars Oil and Gas officials. We asked whether they wanted to repeat the tender. Was there enough time? We said we had worked on our documents. We said you have our bid. Then they said they intended to award the contract without the formalities.[35]

When pressed as to the nature of Khatam's employment and funding, Abedzadeh emphasized that the IRGC's military activities and Khatam's construction activities are kept "completely separate" and that only 10 percent of Khatam's labor is derived from IRGC ranks, and the rest consists of subcontractors. As for Khatam's funding, Abedzadeh asserted that the majority comes from Iran's foreign currency reserve. In response to the interviewer's question as to how the company obtained these funds if "the foreign currency reserve account was established so 50 percent would be reserved and 50 percent would be loaned to the private sector, not to the government," Abedzadeh stated, "Others obtain those funds as well. . . . The government does

---

[34] "Iran Press: General Discusses IRGC Role in Engineering, Economic Contracts," *Sharq*, August 13, 2006.

[35] "Iran Press: General Discusses IRGC Role in Engineering, Economic Contracts" (2006).

not do us any favors. We are paid to do our work. We are fined if we do not. Our difference with private companies is that we do not get to spend our profits." However, when asked whether profits from Khatam's construction projects are used to fund defense initiatives, he admitted, "It does help. It helps the development funding the government provides for the armed forces."

## Illicit and Black Market Activities

Parallel to these overt construction activities, the IRGC also controls a vast shadow economy of illicit enterprises that are hidden from public view. Accusations of the IRGC's black-marketeering, like dissent against its monopolization of key business sectors, remains fragmentary and anecdotal. Among the first to level these charges was the reformist cleric Mehdi Karrubi, who, as Speaker of the Sixth Majles under President Khatami, indirectly accused the IRGC of operating 60 illegal jetties in the country without government supervision. Ali Ghanbari, another Majles member, followed suit, arguing that

> unfortunately one third of the imported goods are delivered through the black market, underground economy, and illegal jetties. Appointed institutions [by Supreme Leader Khamenei] that don't obey the [rules of] the government and have control over the means of power [violence]; institutions that are mainly military, are responsible [for those illegal activities].[36]

The abundant availability of banned commodities in Iran, including alcoholic beverages and narcotics, has led to allegations of IRGC involvement in illegal smuggling activities. While there are no independent means of substantiating such allegations, the IRGC is the only organization, it is argued, that could engage in such large-scale trafficking, due to its vast networks and access to countless jetties unsu-

---

[36] Radiofarda, "Sepah, Terrorism, and Militarism Irani dar meidan-e Jahani" (IRGC, Terrorism and Iranian Militarism in the globe), August 15, 2007b; Sazegara (2006).

pervised by the government.[37] Facilities such as the Martyr Rajai Port Complex in Hormuzgan province are reportedly used to export state subsidized gasoline outside the country.

The IRGC is estimated to yield a 200–300 percent profit on such illegal sales. One Majles member recently stated that IRGC black-market activities might account for $12 billion per year. Another parliamentarian suggested that "invisible jetties . . . and the invisible hand of the mafia control 68 percent of Iran's entire exports."[38] Others claim that a high volume of contraband goods enter the country via "illegal and unofficial channels, such as invisible jetties supervised by strongmen and men of wealth."[39] There are also claims that the IRGC facilitates the transfer of alcohol, cigarettes, and satellite dishes across portions of the Iran-Iraq border that it controls.[40]

Yet at the same time, IRGC and Basij forces have been commended for their positive role in fighting illegal smuggling—a further illustration of the institution's multidimensional and frequently contradictory nature. LEF commander Geravand in Kermanshah province thanked the Basij and the IRGC for their cooperation in the recent initiative to step up security, which has resulted in the seizure of over 200 types of weapons, 75,000 "indecent" CDs, 900 satellite dishes, more than 200 kg of various drugs, and more than 44,000 bottles of foreign liquor.[41]

Our canvasing of available open sources and interviews leaves open the question of where the IRGC's profits are going. It is logical to presume, however, that the funds are used for the following:

- personal enrichment of senior officers

---

[37] Radiofarda (2007b); Sazegara (2006).

[38] Open Source Center, "Iran Economic Sanctions, Government Corruption 1-7 Nov 07," *OSC Summary in Persian*, IAP20071119306005, November 1–7, 2007d.

[39] Open Source Center (2007d).

[40] Radiofarda (2007b). See also Sazegara (2006) and Murphy (2007).

[41] Open Source Center, "Iran: Kermanshah Province Highlights, 9–21 Jun," *OSC Summary in Persian*, IAP20070705434001, June 9–July 5, 2007a.

- funding the acquisition of weapon systems, training, and operational and maintenance costs
- development of Iran's non-Persian peripheral provinces
- bribing powerful political and clerical figures so that they do not oppose increases in IRGC political power
- supporting covert activities abroad
- supporting the Iranian nuclear research program, which is supervised by the IRGC
- providing financial support to IRGC veterans and their families, as well as to the families of IRGC personnel killed in the line of duty
- supporting the ongoing enlargement of the Basij by offering stipends and housing allowances to new recruits.

## Public Works

The IRGC may calculate that any dissent or blowback over its growing business profile and illicit profiteering will be offset by the networks of patronage and clientage that it has built with a myriad of companies. Similarly, the Pasdaran's role in spurring rural economic development through public-works projects affords it a clear opportunity to build a base of rural popular support that can counterbalance any opposition from more urban, entrepreneurial classes.

With these imperatives in mind, the IRGC has two objectives in its rural public-works programs. First, the presence of the IRGC or Basij in these areas acts as a preventative security measure and a bulwark against popular uprisings against the state. At the same time, IRGC officials are able to claim that the presence of Basijis provides increased security for villagers in these areas.[42] Second, construction activities help to create a positive image for the Basij and for the IRGC. As mentioned earlier, our interviews with visitors to Iran suggest that this outreach is, in fact, shaping perceptions; in contrast to the favorable views in the provinces, urban Basij are more frequently viewed

---

[42]  IRNA (2007c).

negatively, as enforcers of strict social mores and as the regime's anti-reformist shock troops.

The IRGC often touts its rural projects as the core of its effort to achieve Islamic unity in line with principles of the revolution. Senior Basij officers hold frequent press conferences to praise the efforts of young Basijis in assisting disadvantaged populations. A recent news report commending the IRGC for its work in rural development stated, "Construction is not possible but through cooperation and like-mindedness. Just as they stood shoulder to shoulder with each other during the war, so in peace too, they have to stand shoulder to shoulder."[43]

The IRGC has initiated several large-scale development projects throughout the country in recent years. One such project is the 900-km "peace pipeline" originating in Asaluyeh, Bushehr province, and extending to Hormozgan province and Iranshahr.[44] Not only does the IRGC recruit local individuals from these provinces to work on the pipeline, thus providing local employment, it also generates other projects along the pipeline route, such as road and school building in adjacent villages.[45] Other IRGC-sponsored rural projects, managed under the auspices of the Khatam al-Anbia, include the Kerman-Zahedan railway system, the construction of the Chabahar port in Sistan-Baluchistan, and the development of a system to transfer natural gas from Asaluyeh.[46]

It appears that, since its inception in 2000, the role of the construction Basij has become increasingly important. The majority of smaller rural development operations are generally carried out by the construction Basij in ethnic-minority regions such as the provinces of Sistan-Baluchestan, Ardabil, Zanjan, and East Azarbaijan. In 2001, Supreme Leader Khamenei recommended the formation of the Hejrat

---

[43]  Islamic Republic of Iran Network Television (Tehran), "Iran War Experience at Service of Agriculture and Construction," BBC World Monitoring, August 8, 2007b.

[44]  IRNA (2007c).

[45]  IRNA (2007c).

[46]  Vision of the Islamic Republic of Iran Sistan-Baluchestan Provincial Television, "Iranian Militia Chief Names Commander in Sistan-Baluchestan," FBIS IAP20070524950023, May 23, 2007b.

Plan (Cultural and Constructive Movement) of the construction Basij, a program with a two-pronged approach to development. On the one hand, the program aims to bolster the economic development of impoverished areas by improving infrastructure and local services. At the same time, it is intended to be an indirect vehicle for indoctrination and resisting corrosive foreign influences.[47] Basij commanders in rural provinces have made an effort to extol the virtues of the program and its popularity among young people. Colonel Dezham Khoy, head of the Ardabil Construction Basij, for example, asserted that approximately 8,500 students and other residents had joined the region's Basij unit in 2007 alone. He stated that these numbers correspond to a 50 percent increase in recruitment from the previous year.[48]

According to Basij sources, in just the two months of August and September 2006, the construction Basij managed to establish 1,800 small manufacturing and training units in rural areas of Iran.[49] Brigadier General Mohammad Hejazi has observed that the group became truly effective in 2006, with an estimated 3.2 million recruits.[50] He stated that 14 billion tomans (almost $15 million) had been allocated in the 2007 national budget for increased development activities, as Supreme Leader Khamenei expected more vigorous efforts both in infrastructure and human capital development.[51] Hejazi has expressed optimism that the Basij will continue to enjoy strong governmental support: "Fortunately, the ninth government's position toward the Basij is most favorable and many members of government are active Basij members. We hope that these favorable points of view will help enhance the Basij and its standing in society."[52]

---

[47]  Open Source Center (2007a).

[48]  Ardabil Provincial TV, "Paramilitary Force Works on Construction Projects in Iran's Ardabil," FBIS IAP20070802950066, August 1, 2007b.

[49]  IRNA, "More Than Thirty-Six Percent of Working Women Have a College Education," April 8, 2008.

[50]  Vision of the Islamic Republic of Iran Network 1, "FYI—Commander of Iran's Basij Interviewed on Development Basij Day," FBIS IAP20070510950001, May 9, 2007a.

[51]  Vision of the Islamic Republic of Iran Network 1 (2007a).

[52]  "Commander Says Basij Not to Allow Intimidation by Terrorists," *Javan*, FBIS IAP20070601011003, May 27, 2007.

Increased government funding and support has indeed stimulated the growth of construction Basij activities. Colonel Firuz Jahantigh, head of the construction Basij in Sistan-Baluchistan, recently said that, in addition to the Asaluyeh-Iranshahr gas pipeline and the Zahedan-Bam railway project, the rural Basijis are working with Khatam al-Anbia to complete major projects such as the Chahnimey-e Chaharrom (a fourth water reservoir) and a roadway between Chabahar and Milak (Zabol).[53] Hejazi has estimated that, by the end of 2007, the construction Basij will have volunteered approximately 20 million hours of labor in the form of services and construction projects throughout the country.[54] Many of these activities involve small-scale projects, such as painting school buildings and repairing tables and chairs.[55] Other, more widespread operations include relief efforts in areas affected by natural disasters[56] and health campaigns to inoculate young children.[57]

Government support has also increased efforts to form partnerships with other government and provincial organizations. The local Endowment and Relief Organization in Ardabil allocated 50 million rials ($5,400) to build an Islamic school and 100 million rials ($11,000) to build a potable water pipeline.[58] Other projects, such as the renovation of dilapidated school buildings, are performed in conjunction with the Ministry of Education.[59] In Zanjan province alone, the Basij had slated 202 schools for renovation, as well as a number of recreational facilities.[60] More recently, emphasis has been placed on coordination

---

[53]  Sistan-Baluchistan Provincial TV Zahedan Vision of the Islamic Republic in Open Source Center, "Iran: Highlights: Iranian Military Developments 23–29 November 2007," *OSC Summary in English*, IAP20071203397002, November 23–29, 2007g.

[54]  Vision of the Islamic Republic of Iran Sistan-Baluchestan Provincial TV (2007a).

[55]  IRNA (2007c).

[56]  Open Source Center (2007a).

[57]  Omestad (1998).

[58]  Ardabil Provincial TV, "Ardabil Officials Inaugurate Basij Work Plan," FBIS IAP20070627950072, June 25, 2007a.

[59]  Vision of the Islamic Republic of Iran Network 1 (2007a).

[60]  "Zanjan Islamic Guards Chief Notes Importance of Basij Training Camps," Iranian Labor News Agency, FBIS IAP20070626950077, June 25, 2007.

with provincial offices of the Agricultural Jihad Organization (AJO) to improve the self-sufficiency of rural areas. Commander of the East Azarbaijan province Basij Mohammad Yusef Shakeri stated that Basij work in the agricultural sphere has increased by almost 180 percent since 2006.[61] The head of the province's AJO, Salman Shefa'at, confirmed that Basij assistance in the farming sector was significant, with approximately 40 percent of Basij activities in the province related to agricultural development.[62]

## The Dilemmas of Economic Expansion

Despite the apparent beneficence of its public-works initiatives, the IRGC's economic expansion is fraught with dilemmas. Among the various areas of its domestic ascendancy, its widening business profile probably has the greatest potential to buffet its future trajectory. As we note in our concluding remarks, a comparative inquiry into the development of similar politico-economic military conglomerates in Pakistan and China suggests the potential for internal dilution of the IRGC's corporate cohesion—if not open fractionalization. According to one Iranian-born observer, there are growing tensions within the IRGC about the institution's corporate narrative of a return to the "golden age," e.g., the ideological purity, militancy, stridency, and insularity that marked the postrevolutionary period.[63] Those within the IRGC who critique this perspective, which they undoubtedly regard as antiquated, argue that such traditionalism is fundamentally incompatible with the imperatives of globalization and economic development and integration. In addition, Iran's possible acceptance of globalization and adoption of a liberalized economy may work against the IRGC's busi-

---

[61] "Iranian Resistance Force Involved in Development of East Azarbayjan," Fars News Agency, FBIS IAP20070621950059, June 21, 2007.

[62] "Iran: East Azabayjan Takes Lead in Construction Basij Plan," Fars News Agency, FBIS IAP20070702950129, July 2, 2007.

[63] Comments of an Iranian-born scholar of Iran at a conference sponsored by RAND, October 29, 2007.

ness interests. As an economic organization more interested in monopoly rather than open competition, the IRGC may wish to keep Iran's economy closed off and under its tight control. If this is the case, U.S. and international sanctions may not weaken the IRGC, but instead enhance its formal and illicit economic capabilities.

Certainly, the lack of financial transparency and accountability into Iran's inner economic workings empowers and supports the IRGC's many illicit activities, as well as its control of a shadow economy. But there are also arguments that the IRGC should harness, rather than resist, globalization, with the question of World Trade Organization accession emerging as a key point of debate in Iran.

Another potential risk—one that has not currently manifested itself in a visible way—is increasing backlash by certain sectors of the population, such as traditional merchant elites, companies that lose on bids for contracts, and the like. On this issue, it is important to note that the IGRC's ascendancy to political power, via the 2005 presidential elections and earlier in its assumption of provincial administration posts, was predicated on a platform of populism, personal modesty, and technocratic proficiency. These virtues stood in stark contrast to the perceived corruption, excesses, and oligarchic tendencies of certain clerical factions—particularly those clustered around Ali Akbar Hashemi Rafsanjani and his so-called "oil mafia." As noted by French analyst Frederic Tellier,

> The (Islamic) revolution spawned its own ruling class and its own tribe of oligarchs with no connection to the real population. . . . To the Pasdaran, the people ignored by the shah are now the same people groaning beneath the feet of the mullahs.[64]

As the IRGC moves closer to resembling the economic oligarchy it sought to displace, it ultimately loses much of the initial appeal that ushered it into power. To what degree are segments of the Iranian population aware of this? And have they linked the IRGC's control of the expansive shadow economy with their own worsening economic

---

[64] Frederic Tellier, *The Iranian Moment*, Washington, D.C.: Washington Institute for Near East Policy, February 2006, p. 52.

situation? According to a Western diplomat resident in Iran from 2003 to 2006, this dissent has not transpired:

> There is no bazaari backlash at this point. The general population doesn't know about the IRGC's illegal jetties, the Caspian Sea villas and their Swiss bank accounts.[65]

Part of this ignorance may stem from the IRGC's secretive conduct of business transactions. In other cases, it may result from the broad-based clientage it has cultivated, co-opting private companies as subsidiaries of its umbrella consortiums. Similarly, by mobilizing and militarizing Iranian civil society through the aforementioned levers of indoctrination and training, the IRGC may have achieved some consensus from business elites and citizens seeking upward financial mobility. As noted by Tellier,

> Through its recruitment, selection and socialization process, the Pasdaran now acts as a kind of ideological filter for future conservative leaders in the Islamic Republic. It offers a way to co-opt and become initiated into the financial mysteries of the Iranian regime, which any person of consequence in the system must know in order to defend his or her financial interests.[66]

For their part, IRGC commanders have justified their institution's economic expansion, deploying a diverse set of themes ranging from the memory of the IRGC's role in the vaunted "sacred defense," to its efforts in the postwar reconstruction, to the cost-efficiency of its commercial services, which ultimately benefit the average Iranian. The Iranian constitution is also frequently cited. The deputy director of Khatam al-Anbia, Abdolreza Abedzadeh, for example, clarified in an interview that Iran's constitution allows for the military to operate economic ventures during peacetime.[67] Echoing this, IRGC commander

---

[65]  Authors' discussion with a Western diplomat, based in Tehran from 2003 to 2006, Los Angeles, California, July 18, 2007.

[66]  Tellier (2006, p. 17).

[67]  International Crisis Group (2007).

Safavi defended the economic activities of the IRGC, citing Article 147 of the constitution. He argued that the nation's military forces are required to participate in development and reconstruction activities during peacetime, a task that they are now performing by the direct order of the Supreme Leader. Khamenei's former representative in the IRGC, Ali Saeedi, has also stated that the engineering and construction capabilities the IRGC acquired during the Iran-Iraq War should be used for peacetime development activities:

> The armed forces need a large number of equipment, machinery, and devices during the war efforts that become idle at the peace time. It is normal for countries to use those assets for civilian purposes. Based on this, we have decided that some of the IRGC's engineering capabilities should be used for civilian purposes.[68]

Despite these attempts to justify its economic and business omnipresence, instances of popular dissent against the IRGC have appeared. As an illustrative example, a businessman who lost a bid on a construction project to an IRGC-affiliated company stated to a Western reporter in 2007,

> How can we compete? Why can they offer such an inexpensive price for a civil project like this? A, they have access to cheap assets and equipment owned by the IRGC. B, for unskilled workers they can use the drafted soldier, though we have to pay. C, they are confident that once they win the tender, they can ignore the overruns.[69]

Echoing this theme, in a letter to the government, 29 private contractors protested the seemingly boundless economic activities of the IRGC, writing,

---

[68] "Namayandeye vali faghi dar sepah-e padaran: sepah nabayad abzar-e tashakkolhaye siasi shaved" (Representative of the Supreme Leader to the IRGC: The IRGC should not get involved in politics) (2006).

[69] Murphy (2007).

> Responsibilities [of the military and civilian institutions] are well
> defined in the Constitution. [Moreover] the goal of the "Next 20
> Years' Economic Projection," is to make the government smaller.
> [We ask the question] whether it makes sense economically and
> technically, to award [all the] large scale projects to the military
> or paramilitary organizations?[70]

The most visible instance of criticism against the IRGC's growing
business profile occurred when it forced the expulsion in May 2004
of a Turkish company, Tepe-Akfen-Vie, which was under contract to
operate the newly opened Imam Khomeini Airport. To do this, the
IRGC's air force abruptly shut down the new airport on its first day of
operations, embarrassing Iran internationally as incoming flights were
diverted, straining Iranian-Turkish relations, and hastening the growing impotence of the Khatami administration by forcing the impeach-
ment of his transportation minister. One of the IRGC's reported
motives for closing the airport was that its own engineering firm had
lost out on the airport contract to the Turkish company.[71] In addition,
the IRGC may have sought total oversight over the airport's operations
as a key transportation hub in its illicit smuggling activities.[72]

Perhaps more than any other instance, the IRGC's closure of the
Imam Khomeini Airport illustrates the way in which its economic
interests, along with its expansive indoctrination efforts, can empower
and impel it toward a more explicitly political role. While it has not
quite reached the stage of a political "counterauthority" to other institutions, such as the Office of the Supreme Leader, its power is indis-

---

[70] Behrouz Khaligh, "Tagheerat dar sakhtar jomhouri eslami: gozar az oligarshi rowhaniat
be oligarshi rowhniat va sepsh" (Transformation in the political structure of the Islamic
Republic: A passage from the clerical oligarchy to the oligarchy of the clergy and the IRGC),
July 20, 2006c.

[71] "Iranian Paper Says Airport Controversy Takes Iran's Internal Divisions 'Sky-High,'"
*Iran Daily* (Tehran), FBIS IAP20040510000022, May 10, 2004; "Iranian Paper Says
Iran's Prestige Damaged By 'Embarrassing' Airport Closure," *Iran News* (Tehran), FBIS
IAP20040510000031, May 10, 2004; IRNA, "Iranian Transportation Ministry Denies
Blaming IRGC For Closure of New Airport," FBIS IAP20040831000004, August 31,
2004.

[72] Murphy (2007).

putably rising. At the same time, it growing politicization could force increased pressures on its internal cohesion similar to those resulting from its economic expansion. We will discuss these dynamics in the next chapter.

# CHAPTER SIX

# The IRGC in Politics

Beginning first with its episodic confrontations against reform activists during the Khatami era, networks of active and former IRGC officers began to take on an increasingly political role that enabled the IRGC— by design or by accident—to emerge as a sort of "guardian" for conservatives seeking to displace Khatami supporters from political power. In 2003, former IRGC members or associates took control of numerous city and town councils, paving the way for their entry into legislative politics during the 2004 parliamentary elections. Of 152 new members elected to the Majles in February 2004, 91 had IRGC backgrounds, and a further 34 former IRGC officers now hold senior-level posts in the government. During the June 2005 presidential elections, besides Ahmadinejad, there were three other candidates associated with the IRGC. However, the IRGC is a club of shared experiences, rather than a definition of a particular person's political inclinations and policies. Larijani and Ahmadinejad were both in the IRGC, yet they have very different viewpoints and political "styles."

## The Origins of the IRGC as a Political Force

The IRGC's political involvement, even if at an informal level, seems very much to be an expansion of its original mandate. Ayatollah Khomeini's perception of the political role of the IRGC and the Basij was effectively a continuation of the policies of the shah. At their formation in the early 20th century, the modern military forces of Iran were banned from political participation by Reza Shah Pahlavi. A constitutional ban prohibited military suffrage. This helps to explain the absence of military coup d'etat activities during the 57 years of Pahlavi rule.

The new revolutionary regime used the old military as a base on which to establish itself, and by creating the IRGC, it tried to ensure the loyalty of the armed forces by relying on gradual but ruthless purges. Although Khomeini did allow the military to vote, its political rights and role went no farther than this. According to his official chronicler, Hamid Ansari, Khomeini was clearly opposed to the politicization of the armed forces. On the eve of formally organizing the IRGC, he went so far as to admonish the Pasdaran against taking sides and acting politically: "You must try to prevent political orientation from entering into the ranks of the IRGC, if it did, it would undermine their military orientation."[1] Khomeini also advised all of the country's military forces against politicization:

> I insist that the armed forces obey the laws regarding the preven-
> tion of the military forces from entering into politics, and stay
> away from political parties, groups and [political] fronts. The
> armed forces [consisting of] the military, the police force, the
> guards, and the Basij should not enter into any [political] party or
> groups, and steer clear from political games.[2]

Whether or not Khomeini favored an engaged or an apolitical military force, one can argue that the constitutional role of the IRGC is purely, and even uniquely, political in its essence. The IRGC is defined as the "guardian of the Revolution and of its achievements" (Article 150)—a political as well as military mission. Section 5 of the charter provided by the Revolutionary Council also presaged training of the IRGC in "politico-military" and "ideological" matters.

Today, as the IRGC becomes ever more involved in internal Iranian politics, Ayatollah Khomeini's original views have become the subject of intense debate. Indeed, the issue of whether or not Khomeini

---

[1]   Hamid Ansari, "Framin va vassaya ye saereeh Imam be niroohay ye mossallah" (Imam Khomeini's direct order and testaments to the armed forces), November 26, 2007.

[2]   Ansari (2007).

ordered the IRGC and the Basij to stay out of politics has been a source
of controversy since the end of the Khatami era. Illustrating this, a
speech to members of the Basij by the Friday prayer leader in Mashhad,
the second-largest city in Iran, prompted a broad-ranging debate in late
2007 with the assertion that

> Khomeini did not mean that they should stay out of politics, but
> rather, the Basijis should be active in politics, and to fend off the
> external and the internal enemies. Imam Reza [the eighth Imam
> of the Shi'ites, and one of the most revered and the only Imam
> buried in Iran] was a Basiji himself.[3]

In response to this assertion, reformists and moderates who were
apprehensive about the increasing militarization of the political system
responded with a salvo of essays, replete with numerous quotes from
no less an authority than the late Ayatollah Khomeini. Mohammad
Salamti, secretary general of the Sazman-e Mujahedin-e Enghelab-e
Islami (the Organization of the Islamic Revolution Mujahedin) party,
echoed Khomeini's injunctions, warning sternly against the politicization of the armed forces, stating that this was a betrayal of their
original purpose.[4] Even the grandson of the late Ayatollah Khomeini,
Hassan Khomeini, entered the debate, arguing that the armed forces
and the Basij should stay out of politics.[5]

For its part, the IRGC has also marshaled the authority of
Khomeini to buttress its argument. For example, Mohsen Rezai, the
primary architect of the IRGC and its central commander for 16 years,
wrote,

---

[3]   Raadmanesh, Maaziar, "Imam Reza Was the First Basij," Roozonline.com, November
23, 2007.

[4]   Aftab News, "Officials Should Prevent the Politicization of the Basij," December 1,
2007.

[5]   Hassan Khomeini, "Control-e gheire rasmiye jamee nesbat be khod bozorgtarin amel-e
control-e jamee ast" (Indirect group controls the main instrument for group control), August
20, 2007.

> Once someone had asked Imam [Khomeini] as to why he lends so much support to the IRGC. The Imam had answered "why not?" and the interlocutor had warned him that it may result in staging a coup [if the IRGC became too strong]. The Imam had answered, "It doesn't matter; it stays in the family [if they stage a coup]; as they are our own guys."[6]

The role of the IRGC as a major factor in political affairs increased dramatically since the death of Ayatollah Khomeini, but, as mentioned earlier, it was marked by a period of marginalization and setback during the Rafsanjani era. During this period, the IRGC was compelled to enter a period of forced military professionalization and ideological deradicalization—and this was accompanied by a clear diminution in its political role. The entire process was intended to help the image of Iran's armed forces, enhance the position of pragmatists within the ranks of the military forces, remove the radicals from command positions, and prepare the country for its "Thermidor" period.[7]

By the time Ayatollah Ali Khamenei ascended to the position of Supreme Leader, Iran's internal balance of power began to change. Former allies and the clerical establishment did not appear to be reliable legitimating sources for the new leader, who was originally a junior cleric from the city of Mashhad, bereft of significant theological credentials. Possibly to compensate for this, the new Supreme Leader cultivated a long-term relationship with the armed forces from the earliest days of the revolution, and the IRGC was the greatest beneficiary of the change in leadership. When reformists during the Khatami era appeared to be a threat to Khamenei, the IRGC and, particularly, its Basij force proved to be natural and indispensable allies.

---

6   Mohsen Rezai, "Zendeguinameh" (Autobiography).

7   In the comparative study of revolutions, "Thermidor" refers to the period of relative pragmatism and realism that followed the French Revolution, specifically the coup d'etat of July 27, 1794; the end of the Reign of Terror; and the execution of Maximilian Robespierre.

## Ideological Factionalism Inside the IRGC

Contrary to some analyses, our inquiry into the IRGC suggests that it has never been a monolithic body in terms of its ideological and political outlook. As in any elite military organization, the IRGC's leadership has been adept at enforcing a measure of uniformity among its members that has subsumed more parochial ethnic and geographical types of identity and loyalty. Within the leadership, these unifying tenets can be generally described as corporatist, authoritarian, and populist—all reinforced by significant revolutionary and Islamic content. Where splits do emerge is not so much over the degree of revolutionary fervor or fidelity to the Islamic Republic's ideals, but rather over the *opportunity costs* to Iran's economy, standing, and progress that this approach has inflicted.

The earliest factionalism in the IRGC emerged when Mohsen Rezai succeeded in moving the IRGC's command from the provisional government to the Revolutionary Council's supervision. Members of the Freedom Movement, including Ebrahim Yazdi, Asghar Sabbaghian, and Mohsen Sazegara, simply resigned. Most members of the Sazman-e Mujahidin-e Enghelab-e Islami, including Morteza Elavairi, also broke away from the IRGC. Other radical leaders, such as Abu Sharif, resigned later, simply because they believed that the IRGC was abandoning its ideals. A number of founding members, such as Muhammad Montazeri, were assassinated by the opposition or killed during the war, while in other instances, planeloads of IRGC and regular military leaders crashed mysteriously.

Reassignment or discharge of individuals from leadership positions also could cause friction within the system. For example, the selection of Morteza Rezai as commander of the IRGC by former President Abolhassan Bani-Sadr was rejected out of hand by IRGC top cadres. On another occasion, when a war commander named Abdolwahhab was discharged by Mohsen Rezai, the rank and file nearly revolted against his decision.[8]

---

8    Ali Akbar Hashemi-Rafsanjani, *Besooy ye Sarnevesht* [Towards Destiny], 3rd ed., Tehran: 2007, pp. 383 and 387.

These early instances of sporadic and uncontrolled factionalism established a pattern within the IRGC that continues to this day. Factional rivalries both within the IRGC and between the IRGC and competing political and security organs are currently one of the Islamic Republic's major weak points in the realm of governance. Although they remain frequently subsumed beneath the IRGC's exterior face of ideological uniformity, these tensions have surfaced periodically, often prompted by a key political event that exposes the IRGC's internal fissures—between different factions and between the rank and file and the leadership. Some of these events include the following:

- *The resignation of Ayatollah Hossein Montazeri as the successor to Khomeini.* Arguably the most respected and credentialed cleric in Iran, Grand Ayatollah Hossein Ali Montazeri was one of the leaders of the Islamic Revolution and was designated in 1985 by the Assembly of Experts to be Khomeini's successor as Supreme Leader. Yet Montazeri increasingly came into conflict with Khomeini over Iran's export of the revolution, the execution of dissidents, the fatwa calling for the death of Salman Rushdie, and freedom of speech. In 1989, Khomeini forced the resignation of Montazeri as his successor-designate.[9] To many devoted IRGC members, particularly those from the lower and middle classes, Montazeri was their *marja taghleed* (source of emulation), and his departure from the political scene was widely interpreted as the effective end of the revolutionary era. According to a clerical source close the IRGC, numerous lower-ranking members resigned after this momentous event. Many of them went back to their former professions as ironsmiths, cab drivers, or construction workers.[10]
- *The 1994 Qazvin riots.* In August 1994, violent rioting broke out in the city of Qazvin, the result of ethnic tensions. Locally garri-

---

[9]  For background, see Said Arjomand, "Authority in Shiism and Constitutional Developments in the Islamic Republic of Iran," in Rainier Brunner and Werner Ende, eds., *The Twelver Shia in Modern Times*, Leiden: Brill, 2001, pp. 301–332.

[10]  Telephone interview with an Iranian-born scholar living in Iran, December 20, 2007.

soned Pasdaran were dispatched to quell the unrest, but their commanders, as well as the rank and file, refused to fire on unarmed protestors. This forced the regime to airlift other Basij and IRGC units from outside the region, raising questions about the IRGC's internal security reliability as a *territorial* army, i.e., a force that draws recruits from the communities where it is garrisoned. Ultimately, the incident emphasized that strongly held attachments based on local identity still pervade the IRGC, despite its self-professed tenets of Islamic universalism, not to mention military professionalism.

- *The rise of the reformists under the Khatami presidency.* The ascendancy of the reformists under President Mohammad Khatami after the 1997 presidential elections revealed significant schisms between the rank and file and the IRGC senior leadership, who supported more authoritarian and pro-establishment figures. The IRGC's leadership, siding with Supreme Leader Ayatollah Ali Khamenei, invoked the fear of an upheaval, using the student uprisings of the late 1990s as its justification. The momentum of the anti-authoritarian movement and the extent of youth frustration with the clerical establishment that became apparent at the ballot boxes and in the universities were significant and of deep concern to Iran's more conservative elements, including those within the circle of the Supreme Leader. As a consequence, these concerns brought the Supreme Leader and the IRGC commanders to the conclusion that a counteroffensive was necessary for regime survival. Twenty-four commanders of the IRGC wrote an open letter to Khatami and threatened him with action if he did not maintain stability and peace in the country. Among the signatories were the former and present commanders of the IRGC, Yahya Rahim-Safavi and Mohammad Ali Jafari.[11] On the other side, prominent reformists were also ex-Pasdaran, such as Ali Rabi'ei and Alireza Alavitabar, further highlighting ideological splits in the institution and among its veterans.

---

[11] Gharargah-e Sazandegiye Khatam al-Anbia (Ghorb), homepage.

- *The election of Mahmoud Ahmadinejad to the presidency.* As noted
  earlier, the election of Ahmdinejad was accompanied by a corresponding expansion of the IRGC into Iran's political and economic sphere. But it does not follow that factionalism within
  the IRGC subsided; in fact, just the opposite was true. First, the
  June 2005 presidential elections were themselves an early expres-
  sion of factional splits that had recently intensified. Aside from
  Ahmadinejad, numerous other former IRGC members ran for
  office, most notably Ali Larijani, Mohsen Rezai, and Mohammad
  Baqer Qalibaf. Although they can hardly be termed moderate,
  they have nonetheless emerged as more pragmatic and concilia-
  tory voices. According to some analyses, these candidates may
  have actually been able to claim greater support from within the
  IRGC during the election than did Ahmadinejad. Exacerbating
  these divisions were notable fissures between the IRGC and the
  Basij that marked the election. Indeed, as noted by one observer
  interviewed by the International Crisis Group, "Had Mohsen
  Rezai won, the IRGC would have won. Had Mohammad Baqer
  Qalibaf won, parts of the IRGC would have won. Ahmadinejad's
  supporters chiefly come from the less well-off Basij."[12]

Since ascending to the presidency, Ahmadinejad's administration
has generated more tension within the IRGC over the opportunity
costs of his militancy, provocative statements and behavior, and fond-
ness for brinksmanship. A succession of recent personnel shifts further
reveals what appear to be competing constellations of former IRGC
and Basij commanders. These shifts also reflect an effort by the IRGC
to deflect pressure from other bureaucratic competitors inside Iran's
defense establishment. They include the following:

- *The dismissal of the longtime commander of the IRGC, Yahya Rahim
  Safavi.* Safavi was replaced on August 31, 2007, by Mohammad
  Ali Jafari, reportedly because he failed to take seriously the threat
  of attack from the United States. Safavi, moreover, endured criti-

---

12   International Crisis Group (2007).

cism for the arrest of five IRGC officials in Irbil, Iraq, on January 11, 2007, and the defection of a high-ranking IRGC general, Reza Ali Ashgari, who was also one of the founders of Lebanese Hizballah. Some Iranian analysts have interpreted the move as an intra-IRGC power play, quietly sanctioned by the Supreme Leader. Jafari is reputed to be close to Mohsen Rezai and Mohammad Baqer Qalibaf, while Safavi's openly partisan support for Ahmadinejad was causing dissent within the Pasdaran's ranks.[13]

- *The resignation of Ali Larijani.* The resignation of Ali Larijani, a former IRGC commander, from his post as Iran's lead nuclear negotiator and secretary of the SNSC brought into public view his long-standing disagreement with Ahmadinejad about the course of Iran's nuclear negotiations. What is significant here is that the choice of his successor was likely an attempt by the Supreme Leader to reduce potentially embarrassing public bickering over the nuclear issue among IRGC veterans, even if that meant installing someone closer to Ahmadinejad's outlook. Larijani's replacement, Saeed Jalili, was a longtime Ahmadinejad advisor who had accompanied the Iranian president on his trip to New York. He is also reputed to be a protégé of Mojtaba Khamenei.[14] In nuclear negotiations, he seemed to closely shadow Larijani, with one U.S. observer noting that he was acting as Larijani's "minder."[15] Jalili's views on foreign policy are decidedly closer to those of President Ahmadinejad. In an interview with the hardline *Ansar News*, he argued against "sacrificing principles in the name of pragmatism" and advocated an "aggressive" and "strong" position on foreign policy coupled with reliance on divine assistance.[16] Organization-

[13] Radiofarda, "Taghyir-e farmandeye sepah pasdaran: manshae khareji angizeye dakheli" (Change in IRGC command structure: Foreign force, inside incentive), August 2, 2007a. See also, Vahid Sepehri, "Iran: New Commander Takes Over Revolutionary Guards," *RFE/RL Iran Report*, Vol. 10, No. 28, September 5, 2007.

[14] Authors' interviews in Tehran, 2007.

[15] Open Source Center, "Analysis: Iranian National Security Adviser Stresses Revolution's Ideals," OSC Feature: Iran, FEA20071106398147, November 5, 2007e.

[16] Open Source Center (2007e).

ally, it is important to note that Jalili comes from the ranks of the Basiji commanders, not from the IRGC, further highlighting what appears to be a "Basiji-centric" cast to Ahmadinejad's coterie of advisors.[17]

These replacements, although partially a function of normal bureaucratic infighting and politics, as well as a response to the perception of mounting U.S. pressure on Iran, may also reflect and presage emerging circles of power within the IRGC. Within these new groupings, three former senior IRGC members bear special attention: Rezai, Qalibaf, and Larijani. As an indication of this trio's influence, emerging coalitions of conservative "principlists" who jockeyed for position in the March 2008 Majles election have referred to them as an almost bloc-like triumvirate, with each political party trying to solicit their endorsement and support.[18]

As the former commander of the IRGC over a 14-year period and the current secretary of the Expediency Council, Mohsen Rezai has become a voice of relative moderation. He has long advocated a modest reconciliation with the United States—he served as a negotiator at track two talks in Cyprus—while also critiquing the Khatami administration's diplomacy. His Web site, Baztab, showcased some of the strongest critiques of Ahmadinejad, before it was closed down by order of the government in September 2007. In 2005, Rezai went so far as to challenge the authority of the Supreme Leader, arguing that

---

[17]  It is also significant that the new deputy interior minister, Alireza Afshar, appointed in August 2007, is the former commander of the Basij. In this position, Afshar will oversee the administration of the 2008 parliamentary elections, including the validation and counting of ballots (Vision of the Islamic Republic of Iran Network 1, "Iran: Military Official Replaces President's Advisor as Deputy Interior Minister," IAP20070826950057, August 26, 2007b).

[18]  For example, see "Secretary of Conservative Front on Preparations for Election," *Resalat* (Tehran), FBIS IAP20071227011022, December 20, 2007, p. 3, commentary by Dr. Sadr: "The United Front Had Constructive Talks with Larijani, Rezaei and Qalibaaf." See also, "Prominent Iranian Conservatives Meet to Discuss Election Ties, Unity," *Tehran E'temad*, FBIS IAP20071225950074, December 24, 2007.

"some of the authority" of the Office of the Supreme Leader had been "relegated" to the Expediency Council in 1997.[19]

Similarly, former IRGC officer, SNSC secretary, and lead nuclear negotiator Ali Larijani has been described as comparatively more pragmatic and moderate than Ahmadinejad, with one Iranian commentator praising his entire family—many of whom occupy key political posts—as possessing an "aggressive" but "tolerant and bargaining character."[20] Yet here again, the concept of pragmatism is relative at best. As the head of the Islamic Republic of Iran Broadcasting from 1994 to 2004, Larijani waged a relentless campaign against Khatami supporters.[21] As Iran's nuclear pointman, he famously declared in a March 9, 2007, speech that "any concession on nuclear technology is tantamount to treason."[22] Nevertheless, some sources have reported that his relative moderation—along with that of his political siblings— has recently provoked opposition from more hardline members of the IRGC. A noted instance occurred prior to the May 2007 U.S.-Iran talks in Baghdad, when IRGC opposition reportedly forced the last-minute cancellation of Larijani's brother's participation in the talks with the United States.

Mohammad Baqer Qalibaf, a former IRGC Air Force commander who went on to serve as the mayor of Tehran, also claims an orientation to a more moderate, pragmatic wing of the IRGC. Qalibaf's credentials include war service in the IRGC Air Force and a stint as commander of the LEF, where his popularity grew as a result of his curtailing the

---

[19] "A Stronger Expediency Council?" Rooz Online, October 2, 2005, quoted in Walter Posch, "Iran's Domestic Politics: The 'Circles of Influence': Ahmadinejad's Enigmatic Networks," European Union Institute for Security Studies, October 19, 2005.

[20] Larijani's father is the prominent cleric Ayatollah Mirza Hashem Amoli, his brother Mohammad Javad is an advisor in the Ministry of Justice, and his brother Sadeq is a cleric and member of the Guardians Council. Since leaving his post as SNSC secretary, Larijani has served as the Supreme Leader's representative to the SNSC ("Commentary: Larijani's Resignation Is a Sign of Decline of Conservatives," *Tehran E'temad*, FBIS IAP20071023950111, October 22, 2007).

[21] "State Broadcasting Manipulates Opinion," in Radio Free Europe/Radio Liberty, *RFE/ RL Iran Report*, Vol. 3, No. 18, May 8, 2000.

[22] "Iran's Man for All Crises Bows Out," Agence France Presse, October 20, 2007.

excesses of the vigilante "pressure groups" (such as Ansar-e Hezbollah). His opposition to the radical vigilantes was significant enough to provoke a rare public rebuke from the vigilantes' commander in Mashhad, who attacked what he perceived as Qalibaf's partisanship with student protestors in 2003:

> Mr. Qalibaf, who speaks of security in speeches, had better prevent illegal death anniversary marches in place of confronting the Hezbollah. The path of these people who talk about democracy is apart from ours. They oppose Islam and we are their enemies.[23]

This incident is significant for two reasons. First, it reveals continuing tensions between the IRGC and the vigilante paramilitaries that, while not directly linked to the IRGC, are staffed by former Pasdaran and Basij personnel. Furthermore, it demonstrates that ascent to high political office can, at times, push the occupant toward the political center, a phenomenon not uncommon in other political settings outside Iran. Thus, the ascent of IRGC leaders to civilian office may not be as deleterious as many have thought, as it appears that it can lead to moderating the more extreme ideological and corporatist views of at least some IRGC veterans.

Since leaving his post as LEF commander, Qalibaf fared well in the 2005 presidential elections. His presidential slogan ("Iranians have a right to the good life") may be indicative of his desire to reconcile ideological steadfastness with economic progress, and he has elsewhere made the ideologically startling assertion that Iran needs an Islamist variant of Reza Khan—a reference to the first shah of Iran, who overthrew the Qajar dynasty and implemented a series of broad-ranging socioeconomic reforms.[24] Aside from his relative political moderation,

---

[23] "Iran: Political Figures Comment on Violent Groups, Elections, Other Issues," *Tehran Yas-e Now*, FBIS IAP20031216000015, December 8, 2003.

[24] Iran Press Service, "Iranians Cool to the Presidential Election," *Safa Haeri*, May 17, 2005. In this interview, Qalibaf declared, "I have no program. I had no time for that. But I shall call for accountability by everyone. Go and see what people say in the taxis or at sandwich stands, saying they want a Reza Khan. I shall be a Reza Khan, but of a Hezbollah type."

Qalibaf appears to be an advocate of the IRGC's participation in the global economic order. For example, he reportedly traveled to Zurich at the invitation of a Swiss cement company to explore a business partnership. Underpinning this pragmatism is his well-known desire to mitigate the opportunity costs of the doctrinal rigidity that has informed Ahmadinejad's policies. In late November 2007, for example, Qalibaf was reported to have stated,

> We could achieve our goals at less cost. There is no need to impose extra cost on society, because there are certain methods to respond to the reasonable demands of the people.[25]

However, this does not mean that Qalibaf is a "moderate" in the Western mold. His comments may not only be a result of pragmatism and moderation, but also a way to differentiate him from Ahmadienjad during Iran's 2009 presidential election.

## Possible Future Scenarios for the IRGC

Public pressures resulting from the opportunity costs noted by Qalibaf could conceivably have a significant impact on the future development of the IRGC. Furthermore, broader changes within Iran, far beyond the immediate control of the IRGC, may well force it to evolve in ways that are not immediately self-evident. Given our study's exploration of the various facets of the IRGC's character and performance and its previous roles, we conclude this chapter with three possible scenarios for its future.

### Scenario 1: The Evolving Role of the Supreme Leader and the Eventual Succession to Khamenei

This first scenario forecasts a temptation by segments of the IRGC leadership to influence the appointment of a figurehead Supreme Leader after the demise of Ali Khamenei. With this watershed event, the con-

---

[25] "Persian Press: Tehran Mayor Said to Criticize Government Policies," *Mardom Salari* (Tehran), FBIS IAP20071121004006, November 17, 2007.

trolling and mediating power of Khamenei will be removed, and the elite may clash among themselves over his successor, with no clear favorite emerging. Of the main contenders, Ali Akbar Hashemi-Rafsanjani is himself elderly and unlikely to have a long tenure in office. More importantly, he is deeply unpopular with the IRGC and conservatives such as Ahmadinejad. For their part, younger leaders, such as Hassan Khomeini (Ayatollah Khomeini's grandson) or Mohammad Khatami, the former president, are too moderate for the taste of conservatives within the IRGC and the Qom establishment.

Having no powerful clerical leader capable of achieving the necessary consensus, the IRGC may step in, selecting a pliant figurehead ayatollah as Khamenei's successor. The benefits of such a move to the IRGC are several. It would require no significant shift in the elite structure, and the IRGC would likely calculate that this figurehead leader would continue to support its primacy in Iran's economic sphere and political life. This would give even more leverage to the IRGC than it enjoyed under Khamenei, at the expense of the civilian-controlled institutions and without evident breaching of the constitution.

This scenario is made more plausible by the observation that the next Supreme Leader could be significantly less powerful than Khamenei, whose power has increased since his appointment not because of religious standing or personal charisma, but rather as a result of the vast bureaucracy under his command. However, as the number of contenders (including the IRGC) for power and influence grow, the mediating role of the future Supreme Leader becomes increasingly more complex and potentially untenable.

### Scenario 2: The "Muslim Reza Khan"

Another way for the IRGC to maintain its preeminence in a situation of political turbulence and uncertainty would be to set the stage for the emergence of a leader in a military uniform who would be known for his Islamist zeal and piety and, therefore, acceptable to broad sections of the clergy while at the same time being controlled by the IRGC itself. This process would echo the rise of former Pakistani dictator General Zia ul-Haq. Such a candidate would promise progress, placing less emphasis on Islamism but not completely abandoning it. As noted earlier, this vision has informed the 2005 electoral platform of former IRGC commander and current mayor of Tehran, Mohammad Qalibaf, who came in third after Ahmadinejad and Hashemi-Rafsanjani. The benefit of this approach for the IRGC is that it would continue to hold the reins of power without giving the appearance of having forsaken the values of the Islamic Revolution.

### Scenario 3: The Religious Turkish Option, or a "Coup by Memorandum"

Another possible scenario would be for the IRGC to attempt to run the country without great input from the clergy. If economic deprivation and fatigue with the regime's top-down religiosity and social strictures worsen, the Iranian people might well support a significant course correction in the form of a non-clerical leader. The IRGC at this juncture could step in and, in a manner similar to that of the Turkish military in the past, quietly announce its intention to clean up politics; to eliminate corruption, bribery, graft, and ineptitude—particularly by the clerics; and to end Iran's international isolation. After this de facto takeover, it could initiate a creeping militarization meant to appease the discontented youth, who are a source of great potential instability. The IRGC could launch this from within by gradually relaxing the religious regulations for its members while enforcing greater adherence to military professionalism. Our goal here in postulating these scenarios for the IRGC's future is not so much to offer a prediction, but rather to highlight the range and diversity of tools it can use to both influence political developments in the Islamic Republic of Iran and adapt to changing international and local circumstances.

# CHAPTER SEVEN

# Conclusion: Toward a More Strategic Understanding of the IRGC

Rather than framing the IRGC as a purely military organization marked by mafia-type economic tendencies and a homogeneous ideological outlook, this monograph has surveyed its broad-ranging roles in Iranian society and its emerging internal divisions. Our analysis underscores that the twin poles of commonly held assumptions about the IRGC are both incorrect. The IRGC is neither a corrupt gang nor is it a firebrand revolutionary vanguard with the aim of exporting Iran's revolution across the region. Rather, its vested and increasing interests in the country's economy make it an increasingly conservative force rather than a radical one.

This study has also challenged the Pasdaran's own self-professed mythology of the "sacred defense" of Islamic Republic during the Iran-Iraq War and its unquestioned function as a modernizing force for progress. The IRGC is at its core a multidimensional institution capable of simultaneously cultivating both legitimacy and dissent among various segments of the population. In emphasizing its benevolent, progressive, and technocratic side, the IRGC can point to drug interdiction, rural construction, laser eye surgery, automobile manufacturing, and sports among its many services to Iran. Moreover, its indoctrination efforts and economic expansion can co-opt a range of population segments into its orbit—ranging from business elites to marginalized rural classes seeking upward social mobility. Yet the Pasdaran have also functioned as the repressive shock troops of the revolution, enforcing the government's strict authoritarianism through its paramilitary wing, censorship, and other mechanisms. Moreover, the institution's widening economic activities, which its officials claim are merely an extension of its postwar reconstruction efforts, have displaced the traditional merchant classes and other financial elites.

What the future holds for the IRGC remains to be seen. The IRGC's influence will probably continue to grow as it continues to be a main contender for power after the death of Supreme Leader Khamenei. There appear to be no significant challengers to the IRGC's bid for a position of dominance within Iran's bureaucratic establishment. Yet in evaluating this growing influence, our study yielded an important caveat that holds true for the broader political trajectory of the Islamic Republic. Despite the IRGC's idealized portrait of itself to both its members and to Iranian society at large, the IRGC is hardly immune to the same worldly pitfalls, temptations, challenges, and bureaucratic mutations that seem to undermine revolutionary entities everywhere.

This observation speaks to the larger issue of the questionable exceptionalism and uniqueness of the Islamic Republic of Iran in the international state system. From this, we conclude that the Islamic Republic and the IRGC, in particular, can be profitably compared to similar revolutionary political orders elsewhere and specifically to their military establishments.

## The Utility of a Comparative Approach: Pakistan and China

As a military organization with substantial and growing interests in the civilian commercial and economic sphere, the IRGC is not unique. Even in the era of the modern nation-state, there are few governments that can fully subsidize their armed forces. In many countries, militaries are encouraged or even required to pursue self-sustaining economic activities to alleviate the resource burden on the general population and excessive funding demands on the central government. Furthermore, the inherent allure of militaries as engines of domestic economic and technical progress is well known and has been studied extensively. This is particularly the case in the context of the Middle East, where the populist image of the "man on horseback" helped to underwrite the anti–status quo legitimacy of the Free Officers in Egypt, the rise of Kamal Ataturk in Turkey, the ascent to power of Mohammad Reza Shah Pahlavi in Iran, the nationalist regime of Abd al-Karim Qasim in Iraq, and others.[1]

The question of time however, provides a significant challenge to the IRGC. As the institution grows in power and influence, so too do its concomitant resource demands. Thus, the IRGC will undoubtedly have to confront the timeless question that has bedeviled its compatriots in other settings: How long can it sustain its populist image before it is seen as having subsumed the corrupt and oligarchic tendencies of the old elite that it replaced? Is there a way in which it can chart an alternative course that balances institutional enrichment with the perception of national progress and modernization? Similarly, what effect, if any, will its expanding and increasingly diverse domestic roles, illicit activities, and commercial enterprises have on order and discipline, not to mention meritocracy and traditional military competence? To gain insight into these issues, we suggest undertaking a deeper comparative study that would compare and contrast the economic dimensions of Iran's Revolutionary Guards with comparable militaries in two major powers to Iran's east—Pakistan and China.

In the case of Pakistan, the militarization of the economy (or the economization of the military) has reached such proportions that Pakistani scholar Ayesha Siddiqa has coined the term "Milbus" (military business) to describe the armed forces' expansive reach into the agriculture, manufacturing, construction, and service sectors and the resulting networks of patronage and clientage that attach it to the civilian

---

[1]  A concise discussion is found in Fuad Khuri, "The Study of Civil-Military Relations in Modernizing Societies in the Middle East: A Critical Assessment," in R. Kolkowitz and A. Korbonski, eds., *Soldiers, Peasants and Bureaucrats: Civil-Military Relations in Communist and Modernizing Societies*, London: George Allen and Unwin, 1982, pp. 9–27. For a useful summary of contemporary analyses in the Arab context, see Elizabeth Picard, "Arab Military in Politics: from Revolutionary Plot to Authoritarian State," in Albert Hourani, Philip S. Khoury, Mary C. Wilson, eds., *The Modern Middle East*, Berkeley and Los Angeles: University of California Press, 1993. Also, Mehran Kamrava, "Military Professionalization and Civil-Military Relations in the Middle East," *Political Science Quarterly*, Vol. 115, No. 1, Spring 2000, pp. 67–92.

elite.[2] Although they should not be overstated, the similarities between Pakistan's Milbus and the IRGC are striking:

- The Pakistani military runs the National Logistics Cell, the largest freight-transportation company in Pakistan. Although technically part of the Ministry of Planning and Development, its operations are managed by serving army personnel.
- The military oversees and staffs the Frontier Works Organization, the country's largest contractor, responsible for the construction of roads and toll collection. Under this umbrella organization, there is a vast array of subsidiary companies covering enterprises as diverse as poultry farms, gas stations, bakeries, and commercial plazas.
- The Pakistani military oversees a number of ostensibly charitable "foundations," including the triservice Fauji Foundation, the Army Welfare Trust, the air force's Shaheen Foundation, and the navy's Bahria Foundation. Overall, these foundations oversee more than 100 companies involved in cement and fertilizer production, banking, education, insurance, and information technology. To attract business, these subsidiary companies make no secret of their associations to the military and, indeed, promote them as an advantage and attraction—the military linkage reportedly brings with it a reputation for efficiency.

According to Siddiqa, the principal supporters and constituents of Milbus in Pakistan are precisely those who might logically be assumed to be the strongest proponents of a more liberal, democratic, and free-market political economy—Pakistan's middle classes. This dynamic may be instructive to those who predict a burgeoning popular backlash in Iran against the IRGC's mafia-like empire.

---

[2]  Indonesia, Chile, Turkey, and Thailand are other places where a similar symbiotic relationship prevails. On Pakistan, see Siddiqa, *Military, Inc.: Inside Pakistan's Military Economy*, London: Oxford University Press, 2007. It is significant that the Musharraf government has banned this book and that the author left Pakistan in mid-2007. We thank RAND colleague Peter A. Wilson for the reference to this work. See also "Military, Inc.: The Political Economy of Militarization in Pakistan" (2005).

The PLA offers another potentially fruitful area of comparison, particularly for exploring the trade-offs and tension between the military's financial aggrandizement and its professionalism.[3] Specifically, the decision by the government of Jiang Zemin to force the divestiture of the PLA from all commercial activities in 1998 suggests that the economic symbiosis between civilian elites and military-run business has its limits—particularly when these financial activities are perceived to inflict deleterious and intolerable costs to military competence, modernization, and readiness.

Although the PLA has enjoyed a degree of economic self-sufficiency since its origins in the 1920s and Mao's "Doctrine of Self-Reliance," its actual commercial and business profits underwent a sevenfold expansion between 1985 and 1990. By the late 1980s, its affiliated business firms—numbering roughly 20,000—were dominant in the farming, transportation, information technology, services, and entertainment sectors. In manufacturing, it produced such popular consumer items as bicycles, refrigerators, and televisions.

Yet this expansion was not without consequences, which may hold lessons for anticipating and understanding the future course of the IRGC. Those same factors that ultimately impelled the civilian leadership to curtail the PLA's commercial footprint in China may well be just over the horizon for the IRGC in Iran. They can briefly be summarized as follows:

- *Intolerable levels of corruption.* As noted by David Shambaugh, James Mulvenon, and others, the PLA's expansion into the illicit economy was marked by a corresponding rise in corruption, black-market enterprises such as prostitution, and favoritism to the

---

[3] These comparative insights are drawn from the following works: Evan S. Medeiros, Roger Cliff, Keith Crane, James C. Mulvenon, *A New Direction for China's Defense Industry*, Santa Monica, Calif.: RAND Corporation, MG-334-AF, 2005; Swaran Singh, "The Rise and Fall of the PLA's Business Empire: Implications for China's Military Relations," *Strategic Analysis*, Vol. 23, No. 2, May 1999; James Mulvenon, *Soldiers of Fortune: The Rise and Fall of the Chinese Military-Business Complex: 1978–1998*, Armonk, New York, and London: M. E. Sharpe, 2001; Dongmin Lee, "Chinese Civil Military Relations: The Divestiture of the People's Liberation Army Business Holdings," *Armed Forces and Society*, Vol. 32, No. 3, April 2006, pp. 437–453.

point that "the whole national economy was placed in jeopardy."[4] This had important consequences for the civilian leadership, as these developments had the collateral effect of tarnishing popular images of the Chinese Communist Party, which in the early 1990s, was trying to enhance its legitimacy based on a platform of anticorruption.

- *The growing regionalization of the economy.* The military's business ventures were becoming increasingly decentralized and provincially based, raising fears within the central government in Beijing of a return to the regional autonomy of the prerevolutionary warlord era.
- *The corrosive effect on military readiness and modernization.* The professionalization and meritocracy of the military was ultimately undermined by the distractions of its financial pursuits. The connections required to secure a coveted position running a PLA-owned business, the logistical energy devoted to smuggling, and the preference for management acumen over battlefield expertise all incurred significant costs in the realm of military competency and lost opportunities for modernization.

Of course, the decision to terminate the PLA's commercial endeavors with the Divestiture Act of 1998 was ultimately rooted in the ascendancy of a more pragmatic and technocratic strand in the civilian leadership's inner circle.

As we have seen, this tension between dogmatism and pragmatism is an omnipresent theme within Iranian political culture and raises the question of whether the greatest challenges to the IRGC's future might actually originate *within* the institution itself—specifically, the potential for greater fissures and factionalism over questions of ideological purity, institutional privilege, and national interest.

---

[4]   Lee (2006, p. 448).

# Business Organizations Affiliated with the IRGC or Influenced by IRGC Personnel

### Khatam al-Anbia

Khatam al-Anbia functions as the IRGC's engineering arm. The organization conducts a range of civil engineering activities, such as road and dam construction and the manufacture of pipelines to transport water, oil, and gas across the country. Khatam is also involved in mining operations, agriculture, and telecommunications.

### Hara Company and Sepasad Engineering Company

Khatam al-Anbia maintains multiple subsidiaries, two of which are Hara Company and Sepasad Engineering Company. Both subsidiaries specialize in excavation and tunnel construction.

### Ehya Sepahan

Ehya Sepahan is a private-holding company that was established with help from the IRGC. It is based in Isfahan and owns several industrial companies. The company's director is Mostafa Safavi, the brother of former IRGC head Rahim Safavi.

### Bahman Group

The IRGC reportedly holds 45 percent of the company's shares. The group operates an assembly line of Mazda cars in Iran.[1]

### Bonyad-e Mostazafan va Janbazan, or Mostazafan and Janbazan Foundation (MJF), or Foundation of the Oppressed and War Veterans

The MJF was created in 1979 under the leadership of Mohammad Forouzandeh, who was a former IRGC official. The bonyad is the largest in Iran, with an estimated net worth of over $3 billion. The MJF reportedly has over 200,000 employees and 350 affiliated companies. It is a state-owned foundation that represented approximately 10 percent of the Iranian government's annual budget in 2003.[2] The MJF provides medical care and recreation for Iran's veteran population. The organization also has a variety of business interests, both in Iran and abroad, including agriculture, industries and mines, civil development and construction, transportation and commerce, and tourism.[3]

### Bonyad Shahid va Omur-e Janbazan, or Foundation of Martyrs and Veterans Affairs

The Bonyad Shahid is a governmental entity that receives its funding directly from the national budget. Former IRGC Air Force commander Hossein Dehghan acts as president and director of Shahid and also serves as an advisor to President Ahmadinejad. Shahid gives home loans to thousands of Basijis and the families of martyrs. It has reportedly loaned 120 million rials to urban families and 150 million rials to rural families.[4] Shahid is also involved in numerous economic endeavors, much like the MJF.

---

[1]  "Malekan-e Saham-e Khodro Dar Burs-e Tehran" (Shareholders of automobile industry in Tehran Bourse), *Hamshahri*, December 20, 2005.

[2]  GlobalSecurity.org, "Bonyad-e Mostazafan va Janbazan," October 5, 2003.

[3]  "Bonyads Ripe for Restructuring" (1999).

[4]  "Iran: Profile of IRGC-Linked Website, Sobhe-Sadegh" (2006).

### Bonyad-e Hefze Arzeshhaye Defa-e Moghaddas, or Foundation of Keeping the Memoirs of Sacred Defense Alive

The Bonyad-e Hefze maintains memoirs, notes, articles, lists of commanders, and lists of Iranian victims of chemical weapons during the Iran-Iraq War. The bonyad is affiliated with the Basij.[5]

### Farhang-e Isaar, or Culture of Self-Sacrifice

Farhang-e Isaar is a governmental project that publishes news, monthly magazines, and books with the goal of promoting the culture of martyrdom and self-sacrifice.[6] The project is controlled by the Council of Coordination and Supervision of the Promotion of the Culture of Martyrdom and Self-Sacrifice and is affiliated with the Basij.

### Bank Melli (National Bank of Iran)

Bank Melli provides a variety of banking and financial services to the IRGC and Qods Force. It is estimated that the bank provided at least $100 million to the Qods Force alone between 2002 and 2006.

---

[5]   Sajed, homepage, no date.

[6]   Farhang-e Isaar, homepage, no date.

# Current and Former IRGC Personnel

This appendix was compiled using open source reporting, which has been cited in the body of the paper. This is not an exhaustive list of current (as of fall 2008) and former IRGC personnel in prominent positions. In addition, some titles and positions may not be current.

## Cabinet

**Mahmoud Ahmadinejad**—President of the Islamic Republic of Iran, former mayor of Tehran, Basij volunteer during Iran-Iraq War
**Saeed Jalili**—Secretary of the Supreme National Security Council and top nuclear negotiator (replacing Ali Larijani), former Basij commander
**Ali Larijani**—Expediency Council member, former IRGC member, former head of state TV and radio, former SNSC representative to Khamenei
**Abdolreza Mesri**—Minister of Welfare and Social Security, former director of the Cooperative Office of the IRGC in Western Iran
**Mohammad Hoseyn Saffar-Harandi**—Minister of Islamic Culture and Guidance, former IRGC deputy commander of Hormozgan province, 1980–1981; former national regional deputy commander of IRGC, 1981–1983; director of the Political Office of the IRGC, 1989–1993
**Mostafa Mohammad Najjar**—Minister of Defense and Armed Forces Logistics; in General Command of Central Headquarters of IRGC Sistan va Baluchestan province; in charge of the Cooperative Office of

the IRGC, 1981; former deputy director of the Warfare Group of the Ministry of the Guards Corps (Vezarat-e Sepah); member of IRGC since late 1979; membership in the board of directors of the Guards Corps Industries; creation of the Training, Treatment, and Equipment Center of the Guards Corps Hospital

**Ali Reza Tahmasebi**—Minister of Industries and Mines, former researcher for defense projects of the Khatam al-Anbia Station of the Guards Corps, 1985–1987

**Seyyed Masud Mirkazemi**—Minister of Commerce, former director of the Center for Basic Studies of the Guards Corps, 2002–2004.

**Seyyed Parviz Fattah**—Minister of Energy, formerly of the IRGC

**Ali Reza Tahmasebi**—Minister of Industries and Mines, formerly of the IRGC

**Seyyed Masud Mirkazemi**—Minister of Commerce, formerly of the IRGC

**Seyyed Parviz Fattah**—Minister of Energy, former deputy head of IRGC-affiliated construction company Sepasad

**Hoseyn Dehghan**—Deputy to the president and director of the Bonyad-e Shahid va Omur-e Isargaran (Foundation for the Martyrs and the Affairs of Self-Sacrificers), former commander of IRGC of Tehran, former acting commander of IRGC of Isfahan (District 2, National), former commander of IRGC of Lebanon, former commander of District 1 of Sarallah and Sarallah Operations Headquarters, former acting commander of the Air Force of IRGC (Niru-ye Hava'i-ye Sepah-e Pasdaran), former commander of the IRGC Air Force, former acting chairman of the joint headquarters of the IRGC, former general manager of the Cooperatives Foundation of the IRGC

**Mohammad Bagher Zolghadr**—IRGC member, recently resigned as Deputy Minister of the Interior; former deputy commander of the IRGC and one of the founders of Ansar Hezbollah

**Hoseini Shahrudi**—Director of the Indoctrination Bureau of the IRGC

## Parliamentarians

**Alireza Afshar**—Deputy Minister of Interior, responsible for the administration of the 2008 Majles (parliamentary) elections, including counting and validating ballots; former Basij commander

## Other Government Officials/Advisors

**Yahya Rahim Safavi**—Assistant and senior advisor to commander-in-chief of Iranian Armed Forces (Khamenei), former IRGC chief
**Mohsen Rezai**—Secretary General of Expediency Council, one of the original IRGC members
**Hojjat ol-Eslam Behzad Jalali**—Recently appointed as Khamenei's new representative in the IRGC
**Sadeq Mahsuli**—Appointed as presidential advisor in 2006; involved in construction, oil, and real estate; former IRGC general who fought in the same division as Ahmadinejad during the Iran-Iraq War

## Mayors/Provincial Governors

**Mohammad Baqer Qalibaf**—Mayor of Tehran, former commander of the IRGC Air Force, former commander of the LEF

## University Chiefs

**Kelishadi**—Head of Amir al-Mu'minin University
**Behrouz Moradi**—On faculty at Imam Hosein University; governor of Hamedan
**Mohammad Mehdi Zahedi**—Head of the SBO at the Science and Industry University
**Mardani**—Head of the Iranian SBO
**Ja'far Ya'qubi**—Head of the LBO

## Bonyad/Media/Business Heads

**Mohammad Forouzandeh**—Director of the Mostazafan and Janbazan Foundation; former IRGC official
**Brigadier General Ehtessam**—Director of Hara Company
**Hossein Shariatmadari**—Director of *Keyhan* newspaper
**Hoseyn Dehghan**—Deputy to the president and director of the Bonyad-e Shahid va Omur-e Isargaran; former IRGC Air Force commander
**Brigadier General Abdolreza Abedzadeh**—Reconstruction deputy of Khatam al-Anbia

## Current IRGC Officials

**Mohammad Ali Jafari**—New IRGC chief
**Brigadier General Qassem Soleimani**—IRGC commander in charge of the Qods Force
**Hosein Salami**—IRGC Air Force commander
**General Manouchehr Foruzandeh**—Director of Information for the IRGC
**Brigadier General Mohammad Baqer Zolqadr**—Deputy Chief of Staff in Basij Affairs; former Deputy Minister of the Interior
**Ali Akbar Ahmadian**—Recently appointed by Khamenei to head the IRGC's Strategic Studies Center
**Sekhavatmand Davudi**—IRGC commander for Rasht province
**Bahman Reyhani**—IRGC commander for Kermanshah province
**Hojjatol Islam Hussein Taeb**—Deputy commander of the Basij
**Mohammad Hejazi**—Joint Chief of Staff for IRGC, former Basij commander
**General Qassem Kargar**—Head of Basij Ashura Brigade
**Khalil Rastegar**—Basij commander in Hormozgan
**General Mehdi Sa'adati**—Basij commander in Khuzestan province
**Dezham Khoy**—Head of the Ardabil Construction Basij
**Mohammad Yusef Shakeri**—Basij commander in East Azarbaijan province

**Majid Fathinezhad**—Basij pilot and head of Basij air units

**Alireza Asgarizadeh**—Commander of Hazrat-e Amir Basij base in Dahaghan (Esfahan)

**Karim Qanbarnezhad**—Basij commander in Ardabil

**Commander Soleymani**—IRGC commander of Basij in "factories, offices, and trades"

**Brigadier General Qolam Reza Ahmadi**—IRGC commander in southern Khorassan

**Colonel Firuz Jahantigh**—Head of Sistan-Baluchistan Construction Basij

**Sa'adati**—Basij commander in Khuzestan

**General Behrouz Esbat**i—Basij cultural deputy

**Colonel Charragh**—Basij acting operations deputy

## Former IRGC Officials

**Mohsen Sazegara**—currently a Harvard research fellow, co-founder of IRGC

**Ali Shamkhani**—Head of the Strategic Investigations Center for Defense Affairs and member of the Foreign Policy Committee, co-founder of IRGC

**Mehrdad Bazrpash**—Served as Ahmadinejad's campaign manager during the 2005 election and was then appointed as the president's advisor on youth affairs for the first year of the presidency, former head of Sharif University SBO

**Brigadier General Esma'il Ahmadi-Moqaddam**—Reportedly instrumental in mobilizing IRGC and Basij support for Ahmadinejad during the 2005 election, appointed by Khamenei as commander of the LEF and director of its Drug Control Headquarters; former Basij deputy commander

**Mohsen Rafiqdust (Rafiqdoost)**—Former head of the IRGC and former head of the MJF

**Ezatollah Zarghami**—Director of state radio and television services, including IRIB, the primary state broadcasting service (replacing Ali Larjani); former IRGC member

# Evolution of the Islamic Republic and the IRGC

Figure C.1 on the following pages presents a timeline of important events for the Islamic Republic of Iran (the top half of the figure) and the IRGC (the bottom half of the figure).

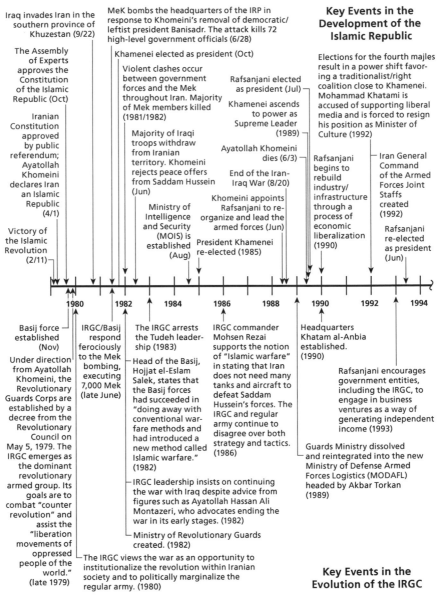

**Key Events in the Development of the Islamic Republic**

**Key Events in the Evolution of the IRGC**

RAND *MG821-C.1a*

**Key Events in the
Development of the
Islamic Republic**

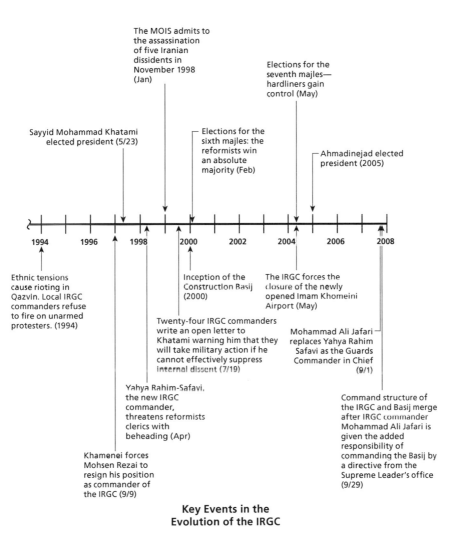

The MOIS admits to
the assassination
of five Iranian
dissidents in
November 1998
(Jan)

Elections for the
seventh majles—
hardliners gain
control (May)

Sayyid Mohammad Khatami
elected president (5/23)

Elections for the
sixth majles: the
reformists win
an absolute
majority (Feb)

Ahmadinejad elected
president (2005)

1994    1996    1998    2000    2002    2004    2006    2008

Ethnic tensions
cause rioting in
Qazvin. Local IRGC
commanders refuse
to fire on unarmed
protesters. (1994)

Inception of the
Construction Basij
(2000)

The IRGC forces the
closure of the newly
opened Imam Khomeini
Airport (May)

Twenty-four IRGC commanders
write an open letter to
Khatami warning him that they
will take military action if he
cannot effectively suppress
internal dissent (7/19)

Mohammad Ali Jafari
replaces Yahya Rahim
Safavi as the Guards
Commander in Chief
(9/1)

Yahya Rahim-Safavi,
the new IRGC
commander,
threatens reformists
clerics with
beheading (Apr)

Command structure of
the IRGC and Basij merge
after IRGC commander
Mohammad Ali Jafari is
given the added
responsibility of
commanding the Basij by
a directive from the
Supreme Leader's office
(9/29)

Khamenei forces
Mohsen Rezai to
resign his position
as commander of
the IRGC (9/9)

**Key Events in the
Evolution of the IRGC**

# Provincial Map of Iran

**Figure D.1**
**Provincial Map of Iran**

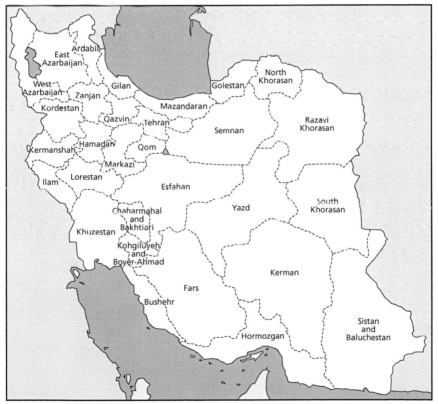

RAND *MG821-D.1*

# Glossary of Persian Terms

**Abadgaran-e Iran-e Islami:** Developers of Islamic Iran
**alghare'eh:** mobile units of the IRGC
**Artesh:** Iran's regular army
**ashura:** male Basij battalion
**bazaari:** member of the traditional merchant class
**Bonyad Mostazafan:** The Foundation of the Oppressed
**Bonyad Shahid va Omur-e Isargaran:** Foundation for the Martyrs and the Affairs of Self-Sacrificers
**Bonyad Shahid va Omur-e Janbazan:** The Foundation of Martyrs and Veteran Affairs
**bonyad:** foundation
**Daftar-e Rahbar:** The office of Supreme Leader Ali Khamenei
**Edareh amaaken:** Office in Ministry of Justice supervising local restaurants, grocery, and retail stores
**fatwa:** religious edict
**Gharbzadeh:** "Westoxified"
**Hezbe E'tedal va Tose'eh:** Justice and Development Party
**Hezbe Kargozaran Sazandegi:** Executives of Construction Party
**Jameeh Rowhaniyyat-e Mobarez:** Association of Militant Clergy
**janbazan:** veterans
**karbala:** a type of Basij special combat group
**komitehs:** committees
**maddahs:** cantors
**Mahdi:** The Imam in Occultation
**Majles:** Iran's national parliament

**Majma-e Rowhaniyoun-e Mobarez:** Society for Militant Clerics
**marja' taghleed:** source of emulation
**moavenat bassazi:** headquarters of reconstruction
**moavenat khodkafaee:** headquarters of self-sufficiency
**nadanan kari:** inexperience
**Pasdaran:** guards
**Sazman-e Harassat:** An IRGC office that functions much like a regular internal security and intelligence office
**Sazman-e Mujahidin-e Enghelab-e Islami:** Organization of the Islamic Revolution Mujahedin
**Sepah-e Pasdaran-e Enghelab-e Islami:** Army of the Guardians of the Islamic Revolution
**shahid:** martyr
**vali faghih:** the supreme jurist
**velayat-e faghih:** The supremacy or the reign of the qualified Shi'ite jurist
**zahra:** female Basij battalion
**zolfaqar:** a type of Basij special combat group

# Bibliography

Abrahamian, Ervand, *The Iranian Mojahedin*, New Haven, Conn.: Yale University Press, 1992.

Aftab News, "Officials Should Prevent the Politicization of the Basij," December 1, 2007. As of October 28, 2008:
http://www.aftabnews.ir/vdcamyn49un0i.html

Ahvaz Vision of the Islamic Republic of Iran Khuzestan Provincial TV, "Iranian Khuzestan Basij Commander Meets Media, Press," FBIS IAP20071122950059, November 21, 2007.

Alavitabar, Alireza, "Nezamian and gozar be Democracy" (The military and the path toward democracy), Web page, 2005. As of December 20, 2007:
http://www.aftabnews.ir/vdcd5nk0yt0o.html

Ansari, Hamid, "Framin va vassaya ye saereeh Imam be niroohay ye mossallah" (Imam Khomeini's direct order and testaments to the armed forces), November 26, 2007.

Ardabil Provincial TV, "Ardabil Officials Inaugurate Basij Work Plan," FBIS IAP20070627950072, June 25, 2007a.

———, "Paramilitary Force Works on Construction Projects in Iran's Ardabil," FBIS IAP20070802950066, August 1, 2007b.

———, "Iran: Volunteer Force to Hold Military Drills in Northwestern Border Province," Open Source Center, FBIS IAP20070812950082, August 10, 2007c.

———, "Iranian Official Praises Student Basij Activity," transcript, FBIS IAP20070831950039, August 30, 2007d.

Arjomand, Said, "Authority in Shiism and Constitutional Developments in the Islamic Republic of Iran," in Rainier Brunner and Werner Ende, eds., *The Twelver Shia in Modern Times,* Leiden: Brill, 2001.

Asadi, Jamshid, "Eghtesad-e Rantkhari Dar Iran" (Rent-seeking economy in Iran), Talashonline, no date. As of October 21, 2008:
http://www.talash-online.com/neshrye/matn_28_0_23.html

Bakhash, Shaul, *The Reign of the Ayatollahs: Iran and the Islamic Revolution*, New York: Basic Books, 1984.

Bashiriyeh, Hossein, *Dibachei bar jamee shenasiy-e Iran* (An introduction to the sociology of politics in Iran), 2nd ed., Tehran: Nashr-e Negah-e Moaser Publications, 2002.

"BBC Monitoring: Iran Media Guide," Caversham BBC Monitoring in English, FBIS IAP20070327950024, March 27, 2007.

BBC News Persian, "Gharardad-e jadid-e tosee-ye meidan-e gazi-e pars-e jonoubi" (Pars Jonoubi new gas contract), May 1, 2005. As of December 20, 2007: http://www.bbc.co.uk/persian/business/story/2005/01/050105_he-ka-gas.shtml

———, "Gharardad-e 1.3 milliard dollari sepah ba vezarat-e naft" (The $1.3 Billion Agreement Between the Guards and the Oil Ministry), May 8, 2006. As of January 28, 2008: http://www.bbc.co.uk/persian/business/story/2006/06/060608_mj-ka-sepah-contract.shtml

"Bonyads Ripe for Restructuring," Middle East Data Project, Inc., Iran Brief 8, December 1999.

Bruno, Greg, "Backgrounder: The Islamic Revolutionary Guards Corps (IRGC)," Council on Foreign Relations, October 25, 2007. As of October 21, 2008: http://www.cfr.org/publication/14324/

Buchta, Wilfried, *Who Rules Iran? The Structure of Power in the Islamic Republic*, Washington, D.C.: Washington Institute for Near East Policy and the Konrad Adenauer Stiftung, 2000.

———, "Iran's Security Sector: An Overview," paper presented at Challenges to Security Sector Governance in the Middle East, Geneva, July 12, 2004.

"Commander Says Basij Not to Allow Intimidation by Terrorists," *Javan*, FBIS IAP20070601011003, May 27, 2007.

"Commentary: Larijani's Resignation Is a Sign of Decline of Conservatives," *Tehran E'temad*, FBIS IAP20071023950111, October 22, 2007.

"Commentary Urges Student Basij to Support Ahmadinezhad Government," *Resalat*, FBIS IAP20070531011001, May 23, 2007.

"Constitution of the Islamic Republic of Iran," English translation, Iranian Embassy, Ottawa, Canada, 1979. As of October 21, 2008: http://www.salamiran.org/IranInfo/State/Constitution/

Cordesman, Anthony H., *Iran's Developing Military Capabilities*, Washington D.C.: Center for Strategic and International Studies, 2005.

"Dam Project Goes to Revolutionary Guards," *Middle East Economic Digest*, October 7, 1994.

Daragahi, Borzou, "In Iran, It's *Supreme* Leader Only Up to a Point," *Los Angeles Times*, December 31, 2007, pp. A1, A4.

Eisenstadt, Michael, "The Armed Forces of the Islamic Republic of Iran," *Middle East Review of International Affairs,* Vol. 5, No. 1, March 2001, pp. 13–30.

"Fact Sheet: Designation of Iranian Entities and Individuals for Proliferation Activities and Support for Terrorism," U.S. Treasury Department Documents and Publications, Federal Information and News Dispatch, Inc., HP-644, October 25, 2007.

Farhang-e Isaar, homepage, no date. As of January 28, 2008: http://www.farhangeisar.net

Farhi, Farideh, "Iran's Security Outlook," *Middle East Report Online,* July 9, 2007. As of October 21, 2008: http://www.merip.org/mero/mero070907.html

Fisk, Robert, "War Wounded Find Comfort from Billion-Dollar Man," *The Independent,* May 26, 1995.

Gharargah-e Sazandegiye Khatam al-Anbia (Ghorb), homepage, last updated February 20, 2007. As of January 28, 2008: http://www.khatam.com/default_english.asp

"Gharardad-e Shirinsaziye gase faze 12 parse jonubi emza shod" (The Agreement on the Sweetening of Gas from South Pars Phase 12 Has Been Signed), *Shana*, November 4, 2007. As of January 28, 2008: http://www.shana.ir/118147-fa.html

Ghouchani, Mohammad, "Etelafhaye rangi: Moghadamei bar etelafhaye siasi dar Iran" (Colorful coalitions: An introduction to the political coalitions in Iran), *Nameh*, May 2006, No. 50. As of January 18, 2007: http://www.nashrieh-nameh.com/articlea.php?mID=34&articleID=/97

GlobalSecurity.org, "Bonyad-e Mostazafan va Janbazan," October 5, 2003. As of January 28, 2008: http://www.globalsecurity.org/military/world/iran/mjf.htm

Green, Jerrold D., Frederic Wehrey, and Charles Wolf, Jr., *Understanding Iran*, Santa Monica, Calif.: RAND Corporation, MG-771-SRF, 2008. As of December 28, 2008: http://www.rand.org/pubs/monographs/MG771/

"Haftomin khate metroye Iran ra sepah misazad" (7th line of Tehran Metro to be built by IRGC), *Keyhan*, April 20, 2006. As of December 20, 2007: http://www.safetymessage.com/npview.asp?ID=1038469

Hajjarian, Said, *Jomhuriyat: Afsunzodai az Ghodrat* (Republicanism: Rubbing off charm from power), 2nd ed., Tehran: Tarh-e No Publications, 2000.

Hashemi-Rafsanjani, Ali Akbar, *Besooy ye Sarnevesht* [Towards Destiny], 3rd ed., Tehran, 2007.

Higgins, Andrew, "As Hard-Liners Rise, Shadowy Revolutionary Guard Muscles in on Airport and Nabs Energy Deals; Dawn Clash Over a Drilling Rig in the Persian Gulf," *Wall Street Journal,* October 14, 2006.

Hiro, Dilip, *The Longest War: The Iran-Iraq Military Conflict,* New York: Routledge, 1991.

International Crisis Group, "What Does Ahmadi-Nejad's Victory Mean?" *Middle East Briefing,* No. 18, Tehran and Brussels, August 2005. As of October 21, 2008: http://www.crisisgroup.org/home/index.cfm?id=3604&l=1

————, "Iran: Ahmadi-Nejad's Tumultuous Presidency," International Crisis Group, *Middle East Briefing,* No. 21, Tehran and Brussels, February 6, 2007. As of October 21, 2008: http://www.crisisgroup.org/home/index.cfm?id=4647&l=1

"Iran: A Fourth of Iranian University Lecturers Are Basij Members," *Javan,* FBIS IAP20070727011008, July 23, 2007.

"Iran: Commander Says Militia Has More Than 12 Million Forces," Vision of the Islamic Republic of Iran Sistan-Baluchestan Provincial TV, FBIS IAP20070523950091, May 23, 2007.

"Iran Clinches Cement Contract," *Middle East Economic Digest,* January 10, 1997.

"Iran: Daily Says Anti-Government University Teachers Increasingly Purged," *Kargozaran* [Executives], FBIS IAP20070826950116, August 25, 2007.

"Iran: East Azabayjan Takes Lead in Construction Basij Plan," Fars News Agency, FBIS IAP20070702950129, July 2, 2007.

Iran Economic News Agency, "Tarh-e LNG 2 va 3 emza shod" (LNG 2 and 3 plans were signed), no date. As of December 20, 2007: http://www.econews.ir/main1.asp?a_id=16672

"Iran: Guards Commander Praises Government's Focus on Islamic Values," *Iran* (Tehran), FBIS IAP20071102950012, October 27, 2007.

"Iran: Political Figures Comment on Violent Groups, Elections, Other Issues," *Tehran Yas-e Now,* FBIS IAP20031216000015, December 8, 2003.

"Iran Press: General Discusses IRGC Role in Engineering, Economic Contracts," *Sharq,* August 13, 2006.

"Iran Press: Student Associations Must Share in University Policies and Decision-Making," *Kargozaran,* September 16, 2007.

Iran Press Service, "Iranians Cool to the Presidential Election," *Safa Haeri,* May 17, 2005.

"Iran: Profile of IRGC-Linked Website, Sobhe-Sadegh," OSC Media Aid in English, GMF20060427388002, April 27, 2006.

"Iranian Official Heralds New Basij News Agency, Weekly," *Keyhan* (Tehran), FBIS IAP20070903950076, September 3, 2007.

"Iranian Paper Says Airport Controversy Takes Iran's Internal Divisions 'Sky-High,'" *Iran Daily* (Tehran), FBIS IAP20040510000022, May 10, 2004.

"Iranian Paper Says Iran's Prestige Damaged By 'Embarrassing' Airport Closure," *Iran News* (Tehran), FBIS IAP20040510000031, May 10, 2004.

"Iranian Resistance Force Involved in Development of East Azarbayjan," Fars News Agency, FBIS IAP20070621950059, June 21, 2007.

Iranian Students News Agency, "Report on Ministry of Intelligence Press Conference." Gooya News, August 31, 2004. As of October 24, 2008: http://news.gooya.com/politics/archives/015502.php

"Iran's Man for All Crises Bows Out," Agence France Presse, October 20, 2007.

IRNA—*see* Islamic Republic of Iran News Agency.

Islamic Republic of Iran News Agency, "Iranian Transportation Ministry Denies Blaming IRGC For Closure of New Airport," FBIS IAP20040831000004, August 31, 2004.

————, "Iranian Paramilitaries Start Drills in East Azarbayjan," Open Source Center, FBIS IAP20070809950061, August 8, 2007a.

————, "Iran: Forty Battalions of Basij Force Carry Out Exercise in Tehran Region," Open Source Center, FBIS IAP20070809950102, August 9, 2007b.

————, "Iran: Guards Commander Says Change in Guards Strategy Necessary," FBIS IAP20070817950094, August 17, 2007c.

————, "Iranian Provincial Commander Calls for More Cooperation with Media," FBIS IAP20070926950125, September 25, 2007d.

————, "Workshop in Ardabil on Reporting About Paramilitary Forces' Activities," FBIS IAP20071114950125, November 14, 2007e.

————, "More Than Thirty-Six Percent of Working Women Have a College Education," April 08, 2008. As of October 28, 2008: http://www.sci.org.ir/portal/faces/public/census85/census85.news

Islamic Republic of Iran Network Television (Tehran), "OSC: Iranian TV Describes Detained Iranian-American Esfandiari as 'Mosad Spy,'" FBIS IAP20070512011017, May 12, 2007a.

————, "Iran War Experience at Service of Agriculture and Construction," BBC World Monitoring, August 8, 2007b.

Jafari, M. A., "The main mission of the IRGC is to deal with the internal enemies," Mizan News, September 29, 2007. As of October 21, 2008: http://www.mizannews.com/default.asp?nid=2386

Jafarzadeh, Alireza, "Islamic Revolutionary Guards Corp (IRGC): Control Over All Aspects of the Iranian Regime," Strategic Policy Consulting, statement National Press Club meeting, August 22, 2007.

Kamrava, Mehran, "Military Professionalization and Civil-Military Relations in the Middle East," *Political Science Quarterly*, Vol. 115, No. 1, Spring 2000, pp. 67–92.

———, "Iranian National-Security Debates: Factionalism and Lost Opportunities," *Middle East Policy*, Vol. 14, No. 2, Summer 2007, pp. 84–100.

Katzman, Kenneth R., "The Pasdaran: Institutionalization of Revolutionary Armed Force," *Iranian Studies*, Vol. 26, No. 3–4, Summer 1993, pp. 389–402.

———, *The Warriors of Islam: Iran's Revolutionary Guards*, Boulder, Colo.: Westview Press, 1993

Khalaji, Mehdi, "Iran's Revolutionary Guard Corps, Inc.," Washington Institute for Near East Policy, *PolicyWatch*, No. 1273, August 17, 2007.

Khaligh, Behrouz, "Changes in the Political Structure of the Islamic Republic: From the Clerical Oligarchy to the Oligarchy of the Clerics and Guards," Akhbar e Rouz, July 4, 2006a. As of November 10, 2008 (in 10 sections):
http://www.akhbar-rooz.com/article.jsp?essayId=4055
http://www.akhbar-rooz.com/article.jsp?essayId=4220
http://www.akhbar-rooz.com/article.jsp?essayId=4435
http://www.akhbar-rooz.com/article.jsp?essayId=4576
http://www.akhbar-rooz.com/article.jsp?essayId=4702
http://www.akhbar-rooz.com/article.jsp?essayId=4844
http://www.akhbar-rooz.com/article.jsp?essayId=4952
http://www.akhbar-rooz.com/article.jsp?essayId=5123
http://www.akhbar-rooz.com/article.jsp?essayId=5317
http://www.akhbar-rooz.com/article.jsp?essayId=5587

———, "Mogheiyate Sepah Pasdaran va Rohaniyat dar sakht-e Ghodrat: Taghyirat dar sakhtar-e siasi-e jomhouri-e eslami, gozar as eligareshi rohaniyat be eligareshi rohaniyat va sepah" (IRGC's position in the power structure of the Islamic Republic: From power of clerics to power of clerics and military), Akhbar-Rooz, July 11, 2006b. As of December 20, 2007:
http://www.akhbar-rooz.com/article.jsp?essayId=4220

———, "Tagheerat dar sakhtar jomhouri eslami: gozar az oligarshi rowhaniat be oligarshi rowhniat va sepsh" (Transformation in the political structure of the Islamic Republic: A passage from the clerical oligarchy to the oligarchy of the clergy and the IRGC), July 20, 2006c. As of January 28, 2008:
http://www.iran-chabar.de/article.jsp?essayId=4435

Khomeini, Hassan, "Control-e gheire rasmiye jamee nesbat be khod bozorgtarin amel-e control-e jamee ast" (Indirect group controls the main instrument for group control), Web page, August 20, 2007. As of January 28, 2008:
http://www.aftab-yazd.com/textdetalis.asp?at=10/20/2007&aftab=8&TextID=19106

Khuri, Fuad, "The Study of Civil-Military Relations in Modernizing Societies in the Middle East: A Critical Assessment," in R. Kolkowitz and A. Korbonski, eds., *Soldiers, Peasants and Bureaucrats: Civil-Military Relations in Communist and Modernizing Societies,* London: George Allen and Unwin, 1982.

Kimmit, Robert," The Role of Finance in Combating National Security Threats," address made to the Washington Institute for Near East Policy's Soref Symposium, May 10, 2007.

Lee, Dongmin, "Chinese Civil Military Relations: The Divestiture of the People's Liberation Army Business Holdings," *Armed Forces and Society*, Vol. 32, No. 3, April 2006, pp. 437–453.

Levitt, Matthew, "Make Iran Feel the Pain," *Wall Street Journal Europe,* July 2, 2007.

"Malekan-e Saham-e Khodro Dar Burs-e Tehran" (Shareholders of automobile industry in Tehran Bourse), *Hamshahri*, December 20, 2005. As of December 27, 2007:
http://www.aftab.ir/news/2005/dec/28/c2c1135767383_economy_marketing_business_bourse.php

Medeiros, Evan S., Roger Cliff, Keith Crane, James C. Mulvenon, *A New Direction for China's Defense Industry,* Santa Monica, Calif.: RAND Corporation, MG-334-AF, 2005. As of January 28, 2008:
http://www.rand.org/pubs/monographs/MG334/

Mehr News Agency "IRGC Commander Takes Charge of Basij Forces," September 29, 2007. As of June 23, 2008:
http://www.mehrnews.ir/en/NewsDetail.aspx?NewsID=561003

Mehrnews, "Farmandehi niruye moghavemate basij be sardar Jafari mohavval shod" (The command of Basij was assigned to Jafari). As of December 27, 2007:
http://www.mehrnews.com/fa/newsdetail.aspx?NewsID=560514

"Military, Inc.: The Political Economy of Militarization in Pakistan," summary of a conference at the Woodrow Wilson Center for International Scholars, June 21, 2005. As of October 22, 2008:
http://www.wilsoncenter.org/index.cfm?fuseaction=events.event_summary&event_id=122809

Ministry of Oil News Agency, "Emza-e Gharardad-e Shirinsaziy-e Gas projey-e Iran LNG" (The contract of gas sweetening of Iran's LNG project was signed), November 4, 2007. As of December 20, 2007:
http://www.aftab.ir/news/2007/nov/04/c2c1194182514_economy_marketing_business_oil_lng.php

"Mobilization Force Demands Halt of Cooperation with IAEA," Fars News Agency (Internet Version), FBIS IAP20070327950047, March 27, 2007.

Mostazafan Foundation, homepage, 2008. As of January 28, 2008:
http://www.irmf.ir/default.aspx

Mulvenon, James, *Soldiers of Fortune: The Rise and Fall of the Chinese Military-Business Complex: 1978–1998*, Armonk, New York, and London: M. E. Sharpe, 2001

Murphy, Kim, "Iran's Guard Builds a Fiscal Empire," *Los Angeles Times*, August 26, 2007.

Nafisi, Rasool, "The Khomeini Letter: Is Rafsanjani Warning the Hardliners?" Iranian.com, October 11, 2006. As of October 21, 2008:
http://www.iranian.com/RasoolNafisi/2006/October/Nuclear/index.html

"Namayandeye vali faghi dar sepah-e padaran: sepah nabayad abzar-e tashakkolhaye siasi shaved" (Representative of the Supreme Leader to the IRGC: The IRGC should not get involved in politics), *Sharq,* July 2006. As of December 27, 2007:
http://www.magiran.com/npview.asp?ID=1144000

National Iranian Gas Company, "Ba hozur-e vazir-e naft va farmandeye kolle sepah-e pasdaran: emza-e moghavelenameye projeye ehdas-e khat lule-e haftom-e sarasari-e gas" (The seventh national gas pipeline contract was signed in presence of the minister of oil and the head of IRGC), June 10, 2006. As of December 20, 2007:
http://www.nigc.ir/Site.aspx?ParTree=111816&LnkIdn=28999

"Nobody Influences Me!" *Time Magazine*, December 10, 1979. As of October 23, 2008:
http://www.time.com/time/magazine/article/0,9171,912545-1,00.html

Nourizadeh, Alireza, "Iran Makes Last Minute Delegation Change Before US Meeting," *al-Sharq al-Awsat*, May 29, 2007.

"Official Provides Details About Internet Filtering," E'ternad (Internet Version), FBIS IAP20070414950102, April 14, 2007.

Omestad, Thomas, "Iran's Culture War," *U.S. News and World Report,* July 27, 1998, pp. 33–51.

Open Source Center, "Iran: Mostazafan va Janbazan Supports Veterans, Covert Activities," May 2, 2006.

———, "Iran: Kermanshah Province Highlights, 9–21 Jun," *OSC Summary in Persian*, IAP20070705434001, June 9–July 5, 2007a.

———, "Iran: Ahmadinezhad Government Reverses Civil Society Gains," Open Source Center Analysis, FBIS IAF20070620564001, June 20, 2007b.

———, "Highlights: Iran Economic Sanctions, Government Corruption 25–31 Oct 07," FBIS IAP20071116306003, *OSC Summary in Persian*, October 25–31, 2007c.

————, "Iran Economic Sanctions, Government Corruption 1-7 Nov 07," *OSC Summary in Persian*, IAP20071119306005, November 1–7, 2007d.

————, "Analysis: Iranian National Security Adviser Stresses Revolution's Ideals," OSC Feature: Iran, FEA20071106398147, November 5, 2007e.

————, "Selection List—Persian Press Menu 17 Nov 07," OSC Summary in Persian, IAP20071117011005, November 17, 2007f.

————, "Iran: Highlights: Iranian Military Developments 23–29 November 2007," *OSC Summary in English,* IAP20071203397002, November 23–29, 2007g.

————, "Iran: Iranian TV Features Basij Parades Across Iran," *OSC Report in Persian*, IAP20071210598001, November 26, 2007h.

————, "Highlights: Iranian Media Developments, November 2007," OSC Summary in Persian, IAP20071205584001, December 5, 2007i.

"Paper Analyses Activities of Political Student Organizations in Iran," *E'temad-e Melli* (Tehran), FBIS IAP20070905950036, September 4, 2007.

Pars Special Economic Energy Zone, "Didar-e Jami az maghamat-e arshad-e sepah pasdaran as tasisat-e parse jonubi" (Visit of IRGC top rank officials from Pars Jonoubi establishments), May 29, 2007. As of January 28, 2008 http://www.pseez.ir/1049-fa.html

"Persian Press: Education Minister Reveals Plans to Make Universities 'Islamic,'" *Sharq*, FBIS IAP20070803011002, July 29, 2007.

"Persian Press: Grand Ayatollah Makarem-Shirazi Urges Exporting Basiji Ideology," *Javan*, IAP20070718011009, July 16, 2007.

"Persian Press: Official Says High Schools Should Have Basij Force Branches," *Marjan*, FBIS IAP20070319005010, February 24, 2007.

"Persian Press: Tehran Mayor Said to Criticize Government Policies," *Mardom Salari* (Tehran), FBIS IAP20071121004006, November 17, 2007.

"Persian Press: University Student Basij Urge President Act Over Studying Abroad," *Nesf-e Jahan*, FBIS IAP20070708011007, June 16, 2007.

Petrochemical Research and Technology Company, Event List, Web page, October 7, 1997. As of October 21, 2008: http://www.npc-rt.ir/eventlist-fa-1386-2-2.html

Picard, Elizabeth, "Arab Military in Politics: from Revolutionary Plot to Authoritarian State," in Albert Hourani, Philip S. Khoury, Mary C. Wilson, eds., *The Modern Middle East,* Berkeley and Los Angeles: University of California Press, 1993.

Pollack, Kenneth M., *The Persian Puzzle: The Conflict Between Iran and America*, New York: Random House, 2004.

Posch, Walter, "Iran's Domestic Politics: The 'Circles of Influence': Ahmadinejad's Enigmatic Networks," European Union Institute for Security Studies, October 19, 2005.

Presidency of the Islamic Republic of Iran, Cabinet of Mahmoud Ahmadinejad, 2007. As of December 20, 2007:
http://www.president.ir/en

"Prominent Iranian Conservatives Meet to Discuss Election Ties, Unity," *Tehran E'temad*, FBIS IAP20071225950074, December 24, 2007.

Raadmanesh, Maaziar, "Imam Reza Was the First Basij," Roozonline.com, November 23, 2007. As of October 28, 2008:
http://www.roozonline.com/archives/2007/11/post_4916.php

Radiofarda, "Taghyir-e farmandeye sepah pasdaran: manshae khareji angizeye dakheli" (Change in IRGC command structure: Foreign force, inside incentive), August 2, 2007a. As of January 28, 2008:
http://radiofarda.com/ArticlePrint.aspx?id=410043

―――, "Sepah, Terrorism, and Militarism Irani dar meidan-e Jahani" (IRGC, Terrorism and Iranian Militarism in the globe), August 15, 2007b. As of December 27, 2007:
http://www.radiofarda.com/ArticlePrint.aspx?id=407336

Radio Free Europe/Radio Liberty, *RFE/RL Iran Report*, Vol. 3, No. 18, May 8, 2000. As of October 21, 2008:
http://archive.rferl.org/reports/iran-report/2000/05/18-080500.asp

―――, *RFE/RL Iran Report*, Vol. 4, No. 6, February 12, 2001. As of October 21, 2008:
http://archive.rferl.org/reports/iran-report/2001/02/6-120201.asp

―――, *RFE/RL Iran* Report, Vol. 6, No. 25, June 16, 2003. As of October 21, 2008:
http://archive.rferl.org/reports/iran-report/2003/06/25-160603.asp

―――, *RFE/RL Iran Report*, Vol. 8, No. 31, August 9, 2005a. As of October 21, 2008:
http://archive.rferl.org/reports/iran-report/2005/08/31-090805.asp

―――, *RFE/RL Iran Report*, Vol. 8, No. 34, August 29, 2005b. As of October 21, 2008:
http://archive.rferl.org/reports/iran-report/2005/08/34-290805.asp

"RAK Unveils Multi-Billion Dollar Plans," *Middle East Economic Digest*, June 3, 2005.

"Rasht IRGC Commander Comments on Basij Goals in Misaq Program," *Rasht Mo'in*, FBIS IAP20070712011010, June 19, 2007.

Rezai, Mohsen, "Zendeguinameh" (Autobiography), Web page, May 8, 2005. As of January 28, 2008:
http://www.rezaee.ir/?p.160

Sajed, homepage, no date. As of January 28, 2008:
http://sajed.ir

Samii, A. William, "Factionalism in Iran's Domestic Security Forces," *Middle East Intelligence Bulletin*, Vol. 4, No. 2, February 2002. As of October 21, 2008:
http://www.meib.org/articles/0202_me2.htm

Sazegara, Mohsen, "Sepah va seh enherof" (The IRGC and three aberrations), July 23, 2006. As of October 21, 2008:
http://www.sazegara.net/persian/archives/2006/07/060723_154435.html

Schahgaldian, Nikola B., and Gina Barkhordarian, *The Iranian Military Under the Islamic Republic,* Santa Monica, Calif.: RAND Corporation, R-3473-USDP, 1987. As of October 21, 2008:
http://www.rand.org/pubs/reports/R3473/

"Secretary of Conservative Front on Preparations for Election," *Resalat* (Tehran), FBIS IAP20071227011022, December 20, 2007

Sepehri, Vahid, "Iran: New Commander Takes Over Revolutionary Guards," *RFE/RL Iran Report*, Vol. 10, No. 28, September 5, 2007. As of January 28, 2008:
http://www.rferl.org/reports/FullReport.aspx?report=571&id=2007/09/571-10-28

Shahrgone, "Vagozari-e ehdas-e khat-e lule-e gaz be sepah bedune anjame tashrifat-e monaghese," no date.  As of January 28, 2008:
http://shahrgone.com/index.php?mode=print&news=1938

Siddiqa, Ayesha, *Military, Inc.: Inside Pakistan's Military Economy,* London: Oxford University Press, 2007.

Silver, Vernon, "The Bank Behind Iran's Missiles," *Bloomberg Markets*, October 2007.

Singh, Swaran, "The Rise and Fall of the PLA's Business Empire: Implications for China's Military Relations," *Strategic Analysis*, Vol. 23, No. 2, May 1999.

*Sobh-e Sadegh,* weekly magazine, November 17, 2007. As of October 21, 2008:
http://www.sobhesadegh.ir/

"Special Report: Iran," *Middle East Economic Digest*, August 24–30, 2007.

"Student Unrest Marks Iran President's University Lecture," BBC World Monitoring, FEA20071008352786-OSC Feature, October 8, 2007.

Teacher's Basij Organization, "Danestanihaye morabiane tarbiati dar tarh-e misaq" (Information for "cultural" instructors in the Misaq plan), no date. As of December 27, 2007: http://www.irantopweb.ir/images/files/farhangiyan/morabiane tarbiati

Technology Development of Iranian Oil Industry, *Negahi be amalkard-e sherkat-e melli naft dar sal-e 1385* (National Iranian Oil Company outlook 2006), 2006. As of December 20, 2007:
http://www.tdca.ir/index.php?page=reporttext&uid=5164

Tehran City Hall Information Management Organization, "Bakhsi az khat-e ahane Tehran Tabriz be zire zamin montaghel mishavad" (Section of the Tehran-Tabriz Railroad Trach Has Been Transferred Underground), February 13, 2007. As of January 28, 2008:
http://www.tehransama.ir/NewsDetail.aspx?NewsID=11208

Tellier, Frederic, *The Iranian Moment,* Washington, D.C.: Washington Institute for Near East Policy, February 2006.

*Towse'eh* (Persian), "Iran: Report Views Positive Change of LEF Towards Students," FBIS IAP20030627000013, June 16, 2003.

"Turkish Firm Signs up for Tehran Airport," *Middle East Economic Digest,* April 30, 2004.

Vision of the Islamic Republic of Iran Network, "Iran Revolution Guards Hold 'Asymmetric Warfare' Ashura-5 Exercises," FBIS IAP20040913000110, September 13, 2004.

———, "IRGC Ground Force Commander Speaks on Reorganization, Combat Plans" FBIS IAP20050309000087, March 9, 2005.

Vision of the Islamic Republic of Iran Network 1, "FYI—Commander of Iran's Basij Interviewed on Development Basij Day," FBIS IAP20070510950001, May 9, 2007a.

———, "Iran: Military Official Replaces President's Advisor as Deputy Interior Minister," IAP20070826950057, August 26, 2007b.

Vision of the Islamic Republic of Iran Sistan-Baluchestan Provincial TV, "Iran: Commander Says Militia Has More Than 12 Million Forces," IAP20070523950091, May 23, 2007a.

———, "Iranian Militia Chief Names Commander in Sistan-Baluchestan," Open Source Center, FBIS IAP20070524950023, May 23, 2007b.

———, "Iran: 'Passive Defense' Contract Held in Southeast," Open Source Center, IAP20080102950084, January 1, 2008.

Vision of the Islamic Republic of Iran West Azarbayjan Provincial TV, "Paramilitaries in Iranian West Azarbayjan Province Attend Training Courses," Open Source Center, FBIS IAP20070726950056, July 25, 2007.

"Website Forecasts Central Bank Chief as Next Victim of Iran's Cabinet Reshuffle," Tehran Baztab, FBIS IAP20070818950092, August 17, 2007.

*Yaletharat,* Vol. 402, November 29, 2006.

*Yas-e Now* (Persian) "Iran: Political Figures Comment on Violent Groups, Elections, Other Issues," FBIS IAP2003121600005, December 8, 2005.

"Zanjan Islamic Guards Chief Notes Importance of Basij Training Camps," Iranian Labor News Agency, FBIS IAP20070626950077, June 25, 2007.

Zibakalam, Sadegh, *Veda ba dovvom-e Khordad* (Farewell with 2nd of Khordad), 1st ed., Tehran: Rouzane Publications, 2003.